Visualising Business Transformation

Business transformation typically involves a wide range of visualisation techniques, from the templates and diagrams used by managers to make better strategic choices, to the experience maps used by designers to understand customer needs, the technical models used by architects to propose possible solutions, and the pictorial representations used by change managers to engage stakeholder groups in dialogue. Up until now these approaches have always been dealt with in isolation, in the literature as well as in practice. This is surprising, because although they can look very different, and tend to be produced by distinct groups of people, they are all modelling different aspects of the same thing. *Visualising Business Transformation* draws them together for the first time into a coherent whole, so that readers from any background can expand their repertoire and understand the context and rationale for each technique across the transformation lifecycle. The book will appeal to a broad spectrum of readers involved in change, whether that is by creating change models themselves (strategists, architects, designers, engineers, business analysts, developers, illustrators, graphic facilitators, etc.), interpreting and using them (sponsors, business change managers, portfolio/programme/project managers, communicators, change champions, etc.), or supporting those involved in change indirectly (trainers, coaches, mentors, higher education establishments and professional training facilities).

Jonathan Whelan is an established business transformation specialist with over 30 years' experience in roles including strategist, architect and programme manager and he has received wide acclaim from organisations globally for his insights. He is the author of *Business Architecture: A Practical Guide*.

Stephen Whitla is the founder and director of Visual Meaning, a management consultancy that helps organisations make sense of change through a combination of systems thinking and visual thinking. Stephen has been working in business transformation for over 15 years. He blogs at www.meaning.guide.

T0371691

"This book is written with clear and direct purpose: to quite literally see how businesses can and should transform. The authors present a thoughtful and compelling argument for modeling change through visualization, and their approach shows rigor, depth, and clarity. In an ever-changing world with increasing complexity, this book is the perfect starting point for visualizing business challenges."

– *Jim Kalbach*, Head of Customer Experience at MURAL
and author of *Mapping Experiences*

"Powerful visual models are the secret weapon of designers, architects and consultants alike. This book gives you not only an extensive selection of versatile models for business transformation, but guides you to choose and weave together suitable models for your challenges: spanning a continuum from abstract maps and real-world illustrations all the way to formal enterprise modelling languages, it will boost your ability to create clarity and move things forward."

– *Milan Guenther*, Enterprise Designer, Author of *Intersection*

"The whole point about the process of business transformation is that it is complex, uncertain and hard to visualise, so the concept behind Jonathan and Steve's book is bang on the money, in terms of relevance and value. The execution is good too. The structure and the thread of the book is intuitive and the writing is excellent. I relish the way the authors interweave their explanations with appropriate and very pertinent references and illustrations, so that the overall effect is very seamless. This is a book that will raise the general literacy around the role, value and shortcomings of visualization so that business people can understand and 'read' these tools and models; distinguish between a model that works and one that isn't very good; and understand why that is."

– *Jonathan Norman*, Knowledge Manager,
Major Projects Knowledge Hub

"Leaders of business transformation often find it hard to describe the changes they want to make in a way that is meaningful to all the different groups of people involved in enacting them. The authors of this book offer some novel insights into the kinds of visualisations that will help different constituencies come to a shared understanding of their new world so that they can work together more effectively in it. They also provide an excellent guided tour around the different types of illustrations and models available and how these help with exploring, designing and communicating change."

– *Sally Bean*, Enterprise Architecture
Consultant, Sally Bean Ltd

"This book is important to all of us striving to build understanding between different disciplines. When we run out of words – as we frequently do – we need diagrams and pictures. This book shows how diagrams themselves can be organised, explaining the different types and their strengths. If you are using diagrams, you need this book."

– *Richard Black*, Chief Data Officer, Danske Bank

"Frank Lloyd Wright observes that 'you can use an eraser on the drawing board or a sledgehammer on the construction site.' You can argue all you want that it takes too long or costs too much to formalize descriptive representations but I will guarantee that if you cannot 'show me the models,' you have NO agreement and you WILL live to regret it! *Visualising Business Transformation* is a very important discussion of Visualization, Models, Diagrams, Abstractions, Agreement and Transformations, etc! These are complex issues that have no simplistic resolution and are not going away. Thank you Jonathan and Steve for your thoughtful discussion."

– *John A. Zachman*, Originator of the Zachman Framework

"This title is a great resource for any architect, analyst, designer, change agent, or anyone else who needs to visually communicate things like 'where we are, and where we want to get to.' There is a lot of fluff about 'visualisation' these days, and pretty 'coffee table' books, but this title makes the principles and methods concrete and actionable. In particular, the 'visualisation continuum' classification is brilliant – it clearly shows how different groups talk past each other, and how to see each other's perspective."

– *Alec Sharp*, Senior Consultant, Clariteq Systems
Consulting and Author of *Workflow Modeling: Tools
for Process Improvement and Application Development*

"This is a definitive guide to visualisation for transformation, from people who really know their craft. I think this is a must-have for anyone who wants better shared understanding, in the right domain, at the right time, in the right way. Every consultant, business student or lecturer, senior leader or transformation professional should have a copy within reach."

– *Benjamin Taylor*, Chief Executive, the Public Service
Transformation Academy and RedQuadrant

Visualising Business Transformation

Pictures, Diagrams and the Pursuit of Shared Meaning

Jonathan Whelan and
Stephen Whitla

Routledge
Taylor & Francis Group

LONDON AND NEW YORK

First published 2020 by Routledge

2 Park Square, Milton Park, Abingdon, Oxon OX14 4RN
605 Third Avenue, New York, NY 10017

Routledge is an imprint of the Taylor & Francis Group, an informa business

First issued in paperback 2022

British Library Cataloguing-in-Publication Data
A catalogue record for this book is available from the British Library

Library of Congress Cataloging-in-Publication Data
Names: Whelan, Jonathan, author. | Whitla, Stephen, author.
Title: Visualising business transformation : pictures, diagrams and the
pursuit of shared meaning / Jonathan Whelan and Stephen Whitla.
Description: Abingdon, Oxon ; New York, NY : Routledge, 2020. | Includes
bibliographical references and index.
Identifiers: LCCN 2019043415 (print) | LCCN 2019043416 (ebook) | ISBN
9781138308244 (hardback) | ISBN 9781315142906 (ebook)
Subjects: LCSH: Business planning–Charts, diagrams, etc. | Organizational
change–Charts, diagrams, etc. | Visual communication.
Classification: LCC HD30.28 .W426 2020 (print) | LCC HD30.28 (ebook) |
DDC 658.4/06–dc23
LC record available at https://lccn.loc.gov/2019043415
LC ebook record available at https://lccn.loc.gov/2019043416

ISBN: 978-1-138-30824-4 (hbk)
ISBN: 978-1-03-233711-1 (pbk)
DOI: 10.4324/9781315142906

Typeset in Optima
by Swales & Willis, Exeter, Devon, UK

To Lindsay and Lizzie
JW

To Julian, fellow traveller on this journey
SW

Contents

Figures

Acknowledgements

Like business transformation itself, this book has been a journey; a journey that has been influenced by our experiences, which collectively span over 45 years. In that time, we have met and worked with very many people, made many friends and achieved many things. We are grateful to all those people who helped us to be who we are and to achieve what we have achieved.

We have been overwhelmed by the enthusiasm, suggestions and insights of colleagues, from the early days when the book was no more than a modest idea, to the point of publication.

We are grateful to Jonathan Norman (in his former role as commissioning editor at Routledge) for recognising the value of our proposal and for providing inspiration and on-going encouragement.

We recognise that these days everyone is extremely busy and time is scarce and that doing something means having to sacrifice something else, especially when that time is volunteered. And that is why we are so grateful to our reviewers: Richard Black, Yorai Gabriel, Milan Guenther, Benjamin Taylor, Sally Bean, Jonathan Norman, Jurie van de Vyver, Adrian Reed, Nick Kemp, Jim Kalbach and Annika Klyver.

Thanks also to Visual Meaning and especially Barbara, Mark and Helen for their insights and contributions, and for enduring our many whiteboard sessions and keeping us focused. Many thanks to Mark Nicoll for producing the cover illustration.

We have acquired examples from many sources, and these have been enthusiastically given and gratefully received. We hope to have acknowledged all sources accordingly.

We are of course grateful to Alexandra Atkinson and her colleagues at Routledge for patiently and diligently guiding us through to the submission of our typescript, and the subsequent transformation of that typescript into this finished product.

Finally, we must acknowledge those who invariably make the greatest sacrifice and provide the greatest support and encouragement, and that is those who are closest to us. For Jonathan, that is Lindsay and Lizzie, and for Stephen, Sarah, Zoe, Emily and Luke.

About the authors

Jonathan Whelan

Jonathan is an established business transformation specialist who has over 30 years' experience within leading organisations in roles including strategist, architect and programme manager. His common sense approach to addressing complex business problems and shaping practical, sustainable solutions has been fundamental to the success of many transformation programmes.

As well as having considerable practical experience he is a Chartered Engineer and a Fellow of the British Computer Society, and he holds numerous industry certifications.

In his spare time, Jonathan writes about business transformation, especially in relation to the issues and opportunities associated with information technology. He is the author of numerous books including *Business Architecture: A Practical Guide* (Gower, 2012) and he has written various articles for industry, corporate and retail publications. Many of his insights and proposals have led to significant programmes of work and he has received wide acclaim from organisations globally.

Stephen Whitla

Stephen is the founder and director of Visual Meaning, a UK-based consultancy that combines systems thinking and visual thinking in support of business transformation initiatives for large organisations and institutions. Visual Meaning exists in a niche between traditional business modelling and pictorial representation, reflecting Stephen's passion for combining creative and analytical skills to make sense of the world.

Prior to founding Visual Meaning, Stephen worked in a variety of change roles at KPMG Consulting before leaving to co-found Delta 7, a more specialised consultancy enabling organisational change through visual dialogue.

Stephen lives in Oxford with his wife, three young children and two cats. He is a fellow of the RSA, a member of the CMI, and regularly teaches visual thinking and system mapping in both academic and non-academic settings. He is a sought-after speaker and writes on meaning and visualisation at http://meaning.guide.

Introduction

Context for the book

As the corporate world changes, so too does the world of 'change' itself. In the past, any significant change would generally involve a large-scale, top-down transformation programme. These large-scale programmes are now often seen as single points of failure. Waterfall is out, agile is in. 'Design' is no longer just a downstream activity driven by strategy – strategy is increasingly led by design *thinking*. Leaders, feeling that they are falling behind the pace of change, are attracted to Scrum practitioners who promise 'twice as much in half the time'. What all these practices have in common is that they put the organisation's users and customers at the heart of the change, designing products, services, processes and ultimately strategy *with* users and customers rather than in isolation from them.

The reason these agile approaches have become popular is that they work! The reason they are controversial is that they only seem to work *consistently* on a relatively small scale. There are plenty of consultancies, frameworks, white papers and blogs proposing the means to scale the 'agile mindset' from teams of ten to organisations of tens of thousands, but the results are, in our experience, too often inconclusive.

Why is this? Why is it that the larger organisations become, the less agile they tend to be? Why do older organisations find it harder to change? There are lots of valid answers involving culture, leadership, clarity of purpose, organisational design, environmental couplings, legacy IT systems and so on. The answer we want to focus on in this book involves *models*, in particular the visual models people create to make sense of change and to describe change, along with the mental models these visuals reflect and inform.

This book is based on two underlying premises:

1   Visual models have the power to create shared meaning;
2   Shared meaning makes businesses more agile.

All organisations want agility, but any agile response presupposes a level of shared understanding and concern among employees and stakeholders as to what needs to happen, when, how and why. We believe that better models have the potential to allow the large organisations of tomorrow to reflect more of the agility of the small organisations of today.

Models break down complexity to help everyone involved and impacted by change get 'on the same page'. Sometimes these models are explicitly written down and distributed, sometimes they are tacitly assumed, and other times they may be unconsciously embedded in the collective psyche, but without being shared *to some degree*, co-ordinated change isn't possible. Or to put it another way: all other things being equal, the winners in a competitive market are more likely to be the companies whose staff have aligned mental models of what's going on and how they are going to respond. It's no use having the perfect solution to a business problem if it only exists in the mind of one person.

This explains why business innovation comes almost exclusively from small organisations, be they start-ups or 'skunkworks' within larger enterprises. If you're in an organisation of a dozen people working side by side, then it's hard *not* to have a detailed shared model of what's going on. Scale this up to 60,000 people and it becomes almost impossible. It's also why design-led approaches have become so popular. If your change process has the customer/user at its heart and involves rapid iterations of ideas and prototypes to solve a problem, then it's very hard as a small team not to have a shared model of what's going on, because the customer is constantly telling you! The problem arises when you need to scale up your solution to be delivered by an enterprise for which that shared model doesn't exist. Shared models will arise organically in any well-functioning small team but, humans being human, that's often as far as they go. For large organisations to match the agility of smaller ones, we need to find ways to create models that travel across silo boundaries.

In this book we review state-of-the-art change modelling, taking in as wide a sample as possible of the different types of models people create to support change, and the eclectic ways that they are used. We look at the organisational paradigms that drive those uses and also drive divisions between the users. Throughout, we are constantly looking to the future and asking, 'Can we do better than this?' If models of change are such a key driver for transformation, then can we not make modelling tools – that is, the software tools that are used to create and maintain models – that are better suited and easily accessible to more people? Can't we design modelling languages that break silos down rather than reinforcing them? At the very least, can't we find ways to be respectful and curious about models that are made by different people and look dissimilar to the ones we might create ourselves?

To answer two possible objections before we start. Firstly, we are *not* saying that shared meaning is the only essential or desirable quality for a model; clearly, they also need to be accurate, relevant, appropriate and so on. What we are saying is that when it comes to achieving *business transformation*, shared meaning seems to be the crucial factor that is most often overlooked.

Secondly, 'shared meaning' does not mean everyone is thinking the same thing! Without a diversity of perspectives and opinions, organisations struggle because they cannot adapt to changing circumstances. The point is that without some shared model of what's going on, divergent opinions themselves make no sense. You may have an ingenious solution to a customer problem, for example, but we can't have a meaningful conversation about it unless we have a shared model of what that problem is.

The role of models and visualisation

Visualisations have been an important method of human communication for at least 35,000 years, from ancient painted drawings on cave walls and ceilings, to the symbols of Egyptian hieroglyphs and the pictograms of Chinese language characters. There are numerous scientific studies that indicate that humans have a better memory for diagrams than for words,[1] a phenomenon sometimes called the 'picture superiority' effect.[2] Certainly, our perception of the world is overwhelmingly visual; we spend half of our mental energy processing visual information.[3]

This is not to say that change should be described in diagrams alone, but clearly diagrams have a fundamental part to play. Any large-scale transformation will only be successful to the extent that it shifts the dominant mental model in the organisation to something new and different, and to do that we need to be able to represent what 'new and different' will look like, and why the status quo is no longer viable. The problem is that 'new and different' in the operation of a business usually refers to content that is non-linear, dynamic and complex which, as we will hopefully demonstrate, is almost impossible to represent succinctly using text alone, as text is linear and static. The medium simply doesn't fit the message.

None of this is to denigrate the value of words! Change is fundamentally about people talking to one another, telling one another stories, making sense of what's going on. But fundamental change involves people not just using words differently, but also using different words. The twentieth-century philosopher Richard Rorty argued that one of the distinguishing characteristics of all truly transformational episodes in human history has been the creation of new vocabularies, not just people arguing better using the old ones.[4] Models are only helpful to the extent that they allow this to happen. Modelling change visually provides a way to engage people in what's going on in a form they can more readily understand and make sense of in their own terms. Change requires that people engage in dialogue, that systems be examined, opinions articulated, options explored, innovation stimulated, designs proposed, uncertainty recognised, feelings expressed and so on. The dialogue that takes place when a model is created or communicated is often where the long-term value is, rather than the reference value of the model itself – as happens, for example, when relationships are established or strengthened between co-workers who attend a modelling workshop.

Like words, visual representations of models are also open to interpretation; the more abstract a model is, the further from reality It is, and the broader the interpretation may be of it – a model of a thing is not the thing itself. The question isn't whether models are right or wrong, it's whether or not they are helpful.

Key propositions of the book

Early in the development of this book we realised that we needed a way to compare and talk about the different types of models that each of us was used to, in a way that was both inclusive and complementary. There is an abundance of model types – or, more specifically, visualisation types – with each having its strengths and drawbacks in terms of accessibility, iconicity,[5] breadth, complexity, familiarity, innovation, variety of uses and audiences, etc. We have not attempted to create a comprehensive catalogue of all the different types of models out there, but rather propose a framework for understanding how they relate to one another.

Our **first proposition** is that all of the visual modelling techniques used in business change can usefully be mapped according to their level of *concreteness* and *constraint*. The resulting graph produces what we will refer to as the **'Visualisation Continuum'**, which is the flow of models running from the top left to the bottom right. This is illustrated in Figure 1.1.

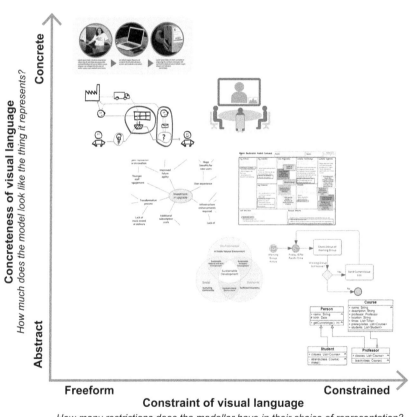

Figure 1.1 The Visualisation Continuum in outline

The horizontal axis of the graph addresses the degree of standardisation of the visual model – from freeform illustrations on the left (which give the modeller a great deal of discretion in how they represent things), through to highly constrained diagrams on the right (which use a formal, standardised notation). The vertical axis addresses the degree of concreteness – from highly abstract models at the bottom (which bear little visual resemblance to the things they represent), through to concrete models at the top (which clearly resemble their subject matter). The resulting Visualisation Continuum gives us a more meaningful way to compare the types of visualisations, the stakeholders that are associated with them and where they are produced in the change lifecycle. We discuss the Continuum in more detail in Chapter 2 and we refer to it throughout the book.

Our **second proposition** is that producers of models in transformation initiatives tend to be drawn towards one end of the Continuum or the other. The Continuum speaks to us of a cultural divide that seems to persist between two sets of communities; namely, those on the bottom right of the diagram who see the world more deterministically (typically programme and technical project managers, enterprise architects, business analysts, software developers) and those in the top left who tend to see the world more emergently (change managers, communicators, entrepreneurs, systems thinkers and designers). We will argue that the types of models associated with each community reflects its (often) unconscious assumptions and biases. Over time, the danger is that each community will come to ignore, denigrate or misrepresent the visual language of the other, resulting in models that generate fragmented rather than shared meaning.

Our **third proposition** is that finding new ways to model that close the gap between the two sets of communities and their associated approaches, methods and software tools, will increase organisational agility by improving shared meaning. We are not suggesting that the Visualisation Continuum needs to be somehow 'shortened', or that visual models need to somehow appeal to a lowest common denominator, but we are suggesting that a lot more could be done if there was more interchange between the two communities. The space on the top right quadrant of the Continuum diagram is conspicuously empty! We see an opportunity for new forms of visualisation that benefit from the rigour and constraints of standards-based approaches, but are more concrete in appearance so as to be more meaningful to more people.

This is all based on our underlying assumption that shared meaning between disparate stakeholder groups improves the efficiency and effectiveness of transformation; in other words, that it will create a better result for less time/effort/cost/risk. Our vision is that more meaningful models could help to make the large organisations of the future as agile as the small organisations of today. The ability to generate shared meaning is clearly not the only thing we need a model to do (it needs to be accurate, manageable, relevant, etc. as well), but we do believe it's the essential characteristic that is most overlooked in the transformation context.

Our motivation for writing this book

We wrote this book for many reasons but there are two primary reasons that drove our collaboration.

Firstly, we both recognise the value that visualisation can bring to change. And we both believe that visualisation in transformation, in fact visualisation in business in general, is a subject that desperately needs more attention and research. Taking us as a case in point, our skills and experiences are from two distinct disciplines: Jonathan from the traditionally structured disciplines of business architecture, enterprise architecture and programmatic change (with their associated methodologies, frameworks and modelling standards – i.e. the bottom right of the Continuum) and Steve from the more emergent disciplines of change management and visualisation (with influences from Systems Thinking, Design Thinking and storytelling – i.e. the top left of the Continuum). Whilst these two fields are complementary, and both are fundamental to the successful delivery of change, the reality is that they are largely practised independently by different communities. This is a shared frustration that we immediately recognised in each other's experiences when we started talking about collaborating on this book.

Secondly, between us, we have spent over 45 years in change-related roles, and in that time we have seen a lot of money invested in change and a lot of that same money wasted on change. And almost everyone in a change-related role will have witnessed this waste. We want to help individuals and organisations to get better at transformation and, in this book at least, we want to do so by specifically addressing the visual representation of change.

We do not promote a specific type of visual (there is not one that satisfies every need), nor do we introduce new ones (there are very many already).

There are resources that focus on strategy, architecture, enterprise modelling, change management, portfolio, programme and project management, business process re-engineering and, more broadly, communication skills. There are also numerous academic studies and conferences, and these are an important contribution to both the art and science of modelling business change. But, at the time of writing at least, we are not aware of any other resource that spans these disciplines with a focus on the visual modelling of change.

Hopefully we provide a balanced view that will help change initiatives to achieve desired business outcomes more effectively and efficiently – this is our intention.

Who the book is for and why

We wanted this book to appeal to a broad spectrum of people, especially those whose role is to create change models (illustrators, graphic designers, visual thinkers, strategists, architects, designers, engineers, business analysts, developers, etc.), as well as business change managers and portfolio, programme and project managers along with change communicators and change champions.

We also wanted the book to appeal to trainers, coaches and mentors who help to hone the skills and competencies of people involved in change, and to higher education establishments and professional training facilities as course material and recommended reading.

Whilst we wanted the book to be a reference point for the various types of models that appear along the transformation journey, primarily we wanted people to look beyond their own discipline and experiences (and associated types of models). We wanted people to explore the other model types and to discover ways to improve the visualisation of business change, increasing shared meaning and, ultimately, making businesses more agile.

How we have organised the book

We have organised the book into three parts as follows.

In **PART I, 'Models and transformation'**, we discuss the purpose and value of models and introduce the Visualisation Continuum as a way of categorising the types of models used to understand and describe change. In this part we also consider modelling in the context of the transformation journey – that is, approaches to change, including deterministic and emergent paradigms utilising agile and waterfall methodologies and the two general communities associated with those paradigms.

In **PART II**, **'A journey along the Visualisation Continuum'**, we take a tour along the Continuum, from the most experiential visualisations through to the most technical, looking at the strengths and weaknesses of each approach. We have structured this part into four broad categories of model: pictures, templates and ad hoc visuals, diagrams and standards-based visuals. At appropriate points along this journey we explore the factors underlying successful models, such as visual resonance, level of detail and the role of facilitation.

In **PART III**, **'Pursuing shared meaning'**, we explore ways that model visualisation can be used to address the divide between the two (deterministic and emergent) communities, and address the proposition that better visuals can help to make the large organisations of the future as agile as the small organisations of today.

We clearly do not have space to address all the different models and modelling approaches in use today! Our intention is not to teach or promote any particular model, but rather to draw attention to the *continuum* that these models exist on. Most readers will probably identify most strongly with only one or two of the models; our hope is that in reading about the other modelling approaches you will be more inclined to cross boundaries, explore the world from other people's perspectives, learn their techniques, and perhaps even think about developing new approaches that break down some of these boundaries even further.

About the examples in the book

Throughout this book we refer to a number of materials from a variety of sources. By referring to these materials we are not necessarily promoting them but we do believe that they are useful reference points.

The numerous example models that we have included reflect a range of visuals spanning the Continuum. As we will see in the next chapter, not all of the visuals we present would traditionally be called 'models', a word associated more with the products of those visuals on the bottom right of the Continuum. We see all of the examples as kinds of model, because they are all attempts to make sense of a complex world. We include examples not to advocate them or to dismiss them but to help us to illustrate a point. They are created using a variety of software tools, some specialist modelling tools and some not, which you may recognise. The inclusion of the examples is not intended to indicate a preference for these tools.

We are, of course, grateful to all sources of the examples and other materials that we include.

About our terminology

In Chapter 2 we define what we mean by a model. However, there are many instances throughout the book where we use the terms *model*, *visual* and *diagram* synonymously. We recognise that this is not strictly correct – a model may, for example, be a mental model or a mathematical model, something that does not take a visual form. However, in general usage the three terms are often used synonymously and so, with a few exceptions in the text, and having recognised the distinction, we are happy to go with the flow rather than being pedantic.

Notes

1 For example, Stenberg, G. (2006). Conceptual and perceptual factors in the picture superiority effect. *European Journal of Cognitive Psychology*, 18(6), pp. 813–47.
2 Shepard, R. N. (1967). Recognition memory for words, sentences, and pictures. *Journal of Learning and Verbal Behavior*, 6, pp. 156–63.
3 Medina, J. (2008). *Brain Rules*. Seattle, WA: Pear Press.
4 Rorty, R. (1989). *Contingency, Irony and Solidarity*. New York: Cambridge University Press (see Part I).
5 How closely the visual resembles the thing it represents.

 **Part I**

Models and transformation

2 Models in context

What do we mean by 'model'?

In general, a model is anything that stands for something more complex than itself. For the purposes of this book, we will be talking about models that are visual representations of organisational systems, and unless otherwise stated, this is what we mean by 'model'.

What is 'modelling transformation'?

When people say they are 'modelling the transformation', what they are usually doing is modelling an organisational system that is undergoing transformation, not modelling the transformation itself. This is an important distinction, as virtually every model created during a change process models a fixed state in that process, not the actual process of change itself.[1] So, a project team might produce a model of the 'as is', the 'to be' and perhaps some stages in between, but in a sense this is not really modelling transformation, because the actual change occurs between these states.

Even when change *is* modelled (as in Systems Dynamics or Agent-based Modelling simulations for example), these are attempts to model how a given system configuration would respond to a given set of circumstances; they generally don't model the change in the underlying system configuration. It's not difficult to build a model that simulates the effect on performance of, say, a warehouse being moved closer to a distribution centre, but each simulation would assume that the change has already occurred. It would be much harder to build a simulation of the actual process of closing the warehouse down and building a new one, which would include negotiating with unions, organising logistics, navigating zoning laws for the new site, and so on.

The closest most organisations get to modelling the change itself is when they create 'roadmap' diagrams, usually for stakeholder engagement purposes, which illustrate the various stages and milestones along a transformation journey. The intention is to turn the abstract content into a story that helps affected people understand what is going to be delivered when, without having to interrogate the detailed plans. Transformation, in other words, is being modelled from the perspective of a stakeholder travelling through time. Even here though, the story tends to be a series of capability descriptions ('by milestone X we will be able to Y'), rather than the organisational changes occurring between the milestones that enable those capabilities.

So, as things stand today, with few exceptions, modelling business change is really about modelling the state of an organisational system at different points in time.

What is a 'system'?

If we are interested in modelling organisational systems, this immediately invokes the next preliminary question, which is: what do we mean by a 'system'? This is not an uncontested question, but we take the word in the broadest sense, to refer to any 'complex whole the functioning of which depends on its parts and the interaction between those parts'.[2]

So, in the context of modelling business change, this 'system' could relate to markets, industries, organisations, people, processes, products, services, technologies (such as computer applications, instrumentation, etc.), and the relationships and interactions between them. It also includes the things which drive or motivate change, or which govern the structure or behaviour of the system such as business goals, business directives (principles, policies) and business rules. To take a systems perspective is to recognise that the behaviour of the whole cannot be understood by analysing any or all of these components *in isolation*, because the behaviour of the whole is an emergent function of the relationships between the parts, not just the parts themselves. As Russ Ackoff wrote:

> Every part of a system has properties that it loses when separated from the system, and every system has some properties – its essential ones – that none of its parts do. An organ or part of the body, for example, if removed from the body does not continue to operate as it did before removal. The eye detached from the body cannot see.
>
> The essential properties of a system taken as a whole derive from the interactions of its parts, not their actions taken separately. Therefore, when a system is taken apart it loses its essential properties. Because of this – and this is the crucial point – a system is a whole that cannot be understood by analysis.[3]

If this was a book about Systems Thinking, we would have to address some vexed questions such as whether systems actually exist in the world or only exist as personal constructs in people's minds. We will talk about the relationship between system models and mental models below, but our reason for using the language of systems is practical rather than philosophical. One of the main reasons that change initiatives fail is the narrowness of perspective of those leading them, for example:

- Investing millions in new capabilities without factoring in the likely responses from other organisations in the surrounding ecosystem;
- Remodelling inefficient processes in isolation, without considering the consequences on parallel processes;
- 'Right-sizing' business units, removing what capacity they had to respond adaptively to unforeseen circumstances;
- Assuming that a technology upgrade will, in and of itself, deliver transformational change.

The systems perspective, by contrast, is always to zoom out and see the higher level, holistic view of the system to understand its emergent properties, to see which relationships give rise to those properties, and to trace those relationships even when they don't fit the neat, straight lines of the organisation chart or the boundaries of the organisation as legally defined. To us, this is the primary reason for learning how to make better models of change and better use of those models; they help us to zoom out and see things in a more systemic way, enabling more meaningful conversations between more diverse groups of stakeholders.

So, modelling business transformation equates to producing visual representations of systems or parts of systems which show intended changes. Typical examples of such models include:

- Business process models;
- Organisational structures;
- Business capability models;
- Software systems;
- Technology landscapes;
- Composite (or hybrid) models that show a mix of elements, such as operating models.

A commonplace perception is that 'real' models of any of these must be constructed based on a standard modelling language, using a notation (a set of predefined symbols and rules) as in the case of process models, enterprise architecture diagrams, organisational charts and so on. While these models are valuable in the right context, they have their roots in an engineering-based view of organisations and organisational change. Such models fail to capture the 'softer' perspective, in which organisations are viewed as ecosystems where context, culture, customer experience and employee attitude are just as significant drivers of the behaviour of the overall system, and in which change is more organic than mechanical. The relationship between the 'harder' and 'softer' side of systems modelling is a constant theme throughout this book.

Meaning and mental models

Most models are not written down, they exist in our minds. Before we even think of creating a Unified Modeling Language (UML) diagram or a rich picture, we are already surrounded by a sea of tacit models in the minds of those around us. The question is not whether or not we have mental models, it's whether those models are any good! Most managers rely on the tacit models they have built up over the course of their careers, and of course someone who has spent a long time working in the same organisation or discipline will probably have a fairly accurate (and therefore valuable) model of how it works, although it will include some inherent bias. Organisations function day-to-day through a matrix of these mental models, which are not explicitly written down and examined, even when there is a formal management system in place.

The problem is, managers' mental models tend to be accurate only for the departments or domains that they have experience of and are responsible for. As soon as a proposed change affects the whole system, conflict arises. Kenneth Boulding described the mental model of the individual (and the compound mental models of social organisations) as 'the image', in his influential 1956 book of the same name. This is an interesting choice of metaphor, chosen to illustrate the fact that what we see in the world is not an objective view of the world as it is, but rather the world as filtered by our image of how we expect it to be, based on past experience; an HR director has a people-centric image of transformation priorities, a CIO has a technology-centric image and so on. The challenge is not that these diverse models exist – there would be a problem if they didn't! The challenge is how they can be connected into an overall vision of the organisation's priorities, where it is going and why.

This brings us to the final term we need to define, which is 'meaning', or more specifically, 'shared meaning'. Meaning describes the feeling we get when something we encounter not only makes sense but also feels important. These two senses (or 'poles'[4]) seem to exist not just in the English word 'meaning', but in the equivalent word in virtually every other language and language family – there is always the recognition of both *signification* ('I get it' – as in 'I see what you mean') and of *significance* ('I care' – as in 'this means a lot to me').

To put it in similar terms to Boulding's in the previous paragraph, meaning is the sense of resonance we experience between our image of the world and the world that we actually encounter. When we see a business visualisation, it needs to express things in a way that is sufficiently familiar to us that we understand it, but if it doesn't say something new or interesting, or allow us to do something we otherwise wouldn't have been able to do, then we don't care. The most meaningful visualisations are those that achieve a balance between the image that we already have in our minds and the image of how things are (or could be) on the page.

When we add to this the idea of 'shared' meaning, we are not saying that everyone can or ought to have the same mental models, but rather that there needs to be some degree of alignment between them for conversation and co-ordination to be possible. We hope through these pages to provoke a discussion about how the images that organisations create on the page can be used to align the images that people have in their minds, so that they can better co-ordinate action, have more meaningful conversations, and accomplish more of what they set out to achieve.

How do we classify models of change?

The first distinction to be made is between *pre-existing visual templates* and *visual modelling approaches*. There are myriad pre-existing conceptual models that get used to support change workshops in which the visual elements are predefined by the model (e.g. Porter's Five Forces, Osterwalder and Pigneur's Business Model Canvas, etc.). The participants in these workshops are effectively populating a pre-existing model. This is hugely valuable, and we will have more to say about it in Chapter 5, but the primary focus of this book is not on visual templates, but on visual modelling as an active process (i.e. where the composition of the model is a product of the modeller(s), not a pre-given structure).

So then, how best do we classify these kinds of models? There is no definitive right way, and for any categorisation, however good, there will be some model types that don't readily fit. Our aim here is not to come up with an ideal, Linnaean classification of all models, but simply to find more useful ways to talk about them. Different models are useful for different purposes, but unless we have a way of describing the differences that are important, we won't get very far with putting them to the best possible use.

There are two main possibilities:

- Firstly, we can classify them by subject, i.e. what they are models *of*. The Business Analysis Body of Knowledge (BABoK)[5] gives an example of this type of categorisation, classifying models as *Rationale, People and Roles, Activity Flow, Capability*, or *Data and Information*;
- Secondly, we can classify them by the *form* they take. The Systems Engineering Body of Knowledge (SEBoK)[6] is an example of this, classifying models as *Formal, Informal, Physical, Abstract, Descriptive, Analytical, Hybrid, Domain-specific* and *System*.

One could argue for a third possibility of classifying them according to their *use* (e.g. exploratory models, stakeholder engagement models, reference models …), but this is a little counter-intuitive, as it is really a classification of change activities rather than models, and the same model could be used for different activities. We'll come to application later, but for now let's explore the first two: categorising by subject and classifying by form.

Categorising models by subject

For the purposes of this book, we categorise the typical subjects of change models as:

- **Motivation** – modelling the justification for change, including the vision, goals and objectives of change;
- **Structure** – modelling change based on the (relatively) static elements that include organisational structures, roles, business capabilities and products;
- **Behaviour** – modelling change based on the dynamic elements of the organisation including business services, business processes and business events;
- **Information** – modelling change from the perspective of the information needs – the data that need to be captured, stored, processed and distributed;
- **Composite** – modelling change using multiple elements (of one or more of the above categories, or indeed any model that doesn't readily fit into one of those categories) and hence the multifaceted nature of business today. The majority of the many models we encounter are composite.

Of course, because all of these subjects are being modelled in transition, the other crucial aspect of the subject being modelled is always **time**. Any of the above models could be created to depict any point in time (e.g. current state, future state, intermediary states), or the dynamic process of change over a time period.

Categorising models by form

Although the subjects of change models are fairly easy to appreciate, classifying their **form** is more problematic. Some models are visual, some are mathematical, some are logical, some are emotional, some are clearly constrained, some are entirely conceptual. Most are a blend.

We suggest that rather than coming up with a fixed set of categories into which model forms have to be pigeon-holed, it's more helpful to see them existing on a set of dimensions that make them easy to compare and talk about. There could be dozens of different dimensions, but we have found the following two to be particularly helpful, and we will return to them throughout the book:

1 **The level of constraint of the visual language**: i.e. how *free* is the modeller in their choice of representation? – see Figure 2.1.

This dimension ranges from creative, freeform and metaphorical representations of transformation objectives and journeys (e.g. whiteboard diagrams, rich pictures, presentation slides) to highly constrained modelling approaches where the visual syntax, format or template has been standardised (e.g. BPMN,[7] UML,[8] SysML,[9] ArchiMate®[10]).

Why is this range important? Because the level of freedom of representation needs to match the level of equivocality of the situation being modelled. Early on in the transformation journey, when the objectives and plan are unclear, you are more likely to be building models to make sense of the situation, explore high-level possibilities and generate fresh ideas. You probably don't want to adopt a modelling approach that forces you to see the world in one particular way. Equally, once you're well down the road into implementation, you want to minimise the possibility of misinterpretation around implementation details, so adopting a standards-based modelling language appropriate for each community involved in delivery makes sense.

2 **The level of abstraction of the visual language**: i.e. to what extent does the model *look like* the thing it represents? – see Figure 2.2.

Freeform   Constrained

Figure 2.1 Freeform vs constrained models

Figure 2.2 Concrete vs abstract models

Ultimately, all visual models are extensions of our mental models, and our mental models are reflections of patterns from our experience. So, it makes sense to think of visual models in terms of how abstract they are, because this helps us predict how easily different audiences will find common meaning in what we have made. Business transformation is a socio-cultural as well as a technical undertaking, so models need to be meaningful as well as accurate in order to be useful. The key question is, meaningful to who? If we want the model to mean the same things to lots of different people then it needs to resemble the common experience associated with those things. Putting an abstract word in a box and using lines to connect it to other words in other boxes presupposes that everyone reads the same meaning into the words. A very technical model in a functional specification may be great for the team of specialists implementing it, but only because they've learned the modelling language in which it's expressed, and they're familiar with the jargon used in it. It's pointless to show it to a group of non-experts if you expect them to do something different as a result.

This is a crucial factor that is rarely discussed, so let's elaborate on what exactly we mean by abstraction. Remember our generic definition of a model as something that stands for something more complex than itself? We said that we use models to make sense of things because the model is simple while the reality is complex. Abstraction is best understood as the relationship between the two – i.e. the amount of complexity captured relative to the simplicity of the model. A simple model representing a complex reality is abstract compared to a complex model representing a simple reality. So 'business capability' is a more abstract concept than 'tree', because the reality it points to is more complex.

Abstraction happens in two ways:

Firstly, we can have abstraction of **concept**. For example, here's a sequence of concepts in decreasing order of abstraction. Each word could potentially refer to the same thing, but at a different level of abstraction, as shown in Figure 2.3.

Each concept uses a single word to refer to a narrower and narrower subset of possible experiences, i.e. it has less complexity. You can't directly see or interact with the concept 'organisation', because it is a label for a set of concepts, whereas anyone familiar with the American sitcom *Friends* will identify Central Perk with a particular coffee shop, with its own collection of characters and events that they have had direct experience of through a television screen.

Secondly, we can have abstraction of **form**. Figure 2.4 shows a word repeated four times in a different visual context.

Once again, notice how from left to right each symbol refers to a narrower and narrower subset of possible experiences as the level of abstraction decreases. Not only does the server symbol on the left have various potential technological meanings (a bare-metal server, a virtualised server, an application server …), but outside of an organisational and technological context it could refer to all sorts of things (e.g. someone who waits at tables, a large spoon for serving food, someone about to hit a tennis ball …). Its abstraction level is high. As we go through the levels of increasing iconicity towards the photograph, the number of possible

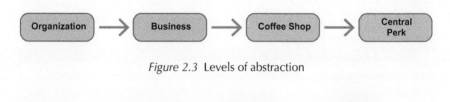

Figure 2.3 Levels of abstraction

Figure 2.4 Visual representations of a server

interpretations drop – a word in a box could represent lots of different objects, whereas an arrow pointing to a particular physical entity could not. Once again, the level of complexity is lower as the abstraction reduces and the representation becomes more concrete.

Why is this useful? Because one way to understand how easily different audiences are going to make sense of your visual model is to appreciate how far removed it is – either in form or in content – from the experiences of each audience group. Express an abstract concept using jargon alone and you create divergent interpretations; express a concrete concept using a picture and you create shared meaning.

It's not that abstraction is good or bad, it's that you need to choose the level of abstraction that's appropriate to the audience and the context. An abstract model supporting a conversation between experts will allow the conversation to cover more ground in the available time, because it can be created and manipulated so much more quickly than a pictorial model in which all the concepts need to be spelled out explicitly. But once you need non-experts to also understand what's going on, the abstract model falls apart, because each person interprets the model, along with your explanation of it, in the way that best reflects their existing mental model: customer service designers might see the word 'service' in a box and assume it refers to customer interactions, IT might see it and assume it refers to an IT service, and HR might see it and assume it refers to a corporate value.

Visual archetypes

Putting these two dimensions together gives us a range of different archetypal visual forms. Before looking at how this plays out in organisational change visualisations, consider a real-world example involving a physical object: Figure 2.5 shows four different visual representations of a steam locomotive by plotting concreteness of form against constraint of visual language.

Starting with the bottom-left box, we have a 6-year-old child's drawing of a steam train, a highly idiosyncratic interpretation. Because the main objective of change visuals is usually to create shared meaning rather than divergent/subjective interpretations, abstract/freeform visuals are rare. There is an interesting question here as to whether creating deliberately abstract representations of business concepts could be useful in the initial

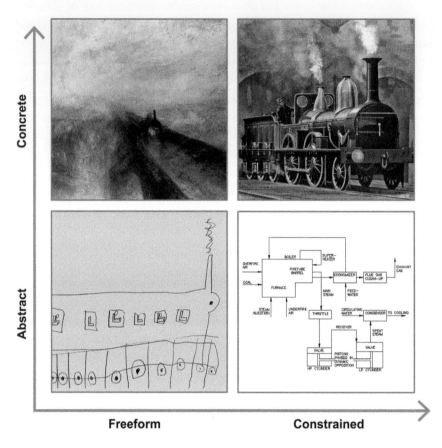

Figure 2.5 Visual representations of a steam locomotive

developmental/exploratory stages of transformation – rather like the Oblique Strategies developed by Brian Eno to enrich the creative process,[11] which inspired so many similar approaches in the design industry. In practice though, once a change process is underway, the problem tends to be more of creating convergent rather than divergent interpretations of what the business is trying to do.

One could argue that a significant proportion of business-as-usual corporate communications activity fits in this box – inasmuch as it uses abstract, generic business words and concepts, branded with the company's visual identity to create a veneer of consistency, but in practice is open to a hundred different interpretations, and is often ignored as a result.

Most people want to know what change will mean to them in a practical, hands-on way, to talk about what needs to be done and how people are going to be affected as a result.

The top-right archetype is also rare because, just like the painting shown, being constrained to a fixed set of standards while also representing the subject in a way that is visually recognisable is very demanding (in terms of both time and skill) to create and maintain.

That leaves the top-left and bottom-right boxes, which is where the vast majority of organisational visualisations reside, and gives us a much more straightforward contrast – between visuals that generate shared meaning because they capture the essence of the things they represent, but lack technical accuracy, and visuals that can represent very complex situations using a constrained visual language, but which are too abstract for a general audience to understand.

The Visualisation Continuum

When we plot the types of visual that are typically used in transformation onto the two-dimensional framework, we do find that the focus is indeed on the freeform/experiential and constrained/abstract archetypes, but that these are two ends of a continuum rather than fixed categories, i.e. the Visualisation Continuum which we referred to in Chapter 1. We have also identified four groupings of visuals along the Continuum, namely: pictures, templates and ad hoc visuals, diagrams and standards-based visuals, which map onto the Continuum as shown in Figure 2.6.

The selection and locations of the various types of visuals on this diagram are subjective on our part, and you will almost certainly have different views based on your experience. The range of types plotted is also not meant to be exhaustive in any way – we have chosen these as representative examples of where different approaches might fit relative to the visual archetypes.

We have found this diagram to be an extremely helpful way of understanding the tensions that need to be resolved when choosing the most appropriate way to model and communicate business change, although in our experience the fact that the choice exists is not something that most people think about. The average project team member has their preferred

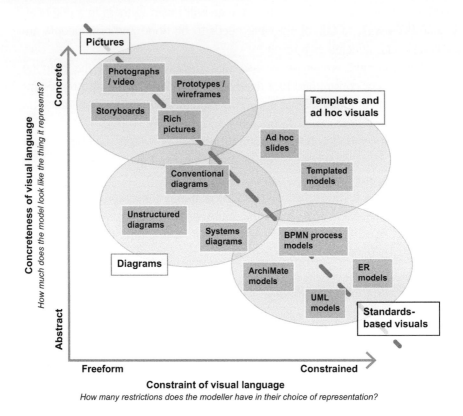

Figure 2.6 Example model types on the Visualisation Continuum

modelling approach, which they use irrespective of its suitability for the audience and situation.

What's most interesting about this, though, is that, as we noted above, no matter how broadly one locates the approaches, there is a clear pull towards the diagonal axis from both the bottom left and the top right, which are fairly empty. This is inevitable. The more concrete a representation, the less constraint is required because the meaning of the symbol is obvious. We do not need a formal grammar to tell us that a subject in a photograph or illustration is a person, for example. But we do if an icon of a cylinder is actually a business role (as in ArchiMate®), as shown in the example in Figure 2.7.

This is like the relationship between hieroglyphics and modern alphabet-based writing. Anyone can have a go at deciphering hieroglyphics,

 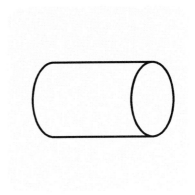

Figure 2.7 Contrasting visualisations of a business role

because they visually resemble the things they represent, but the author is limited in the level of abstraction of what they can say and how precisely they can say it. With writing, on the other hand, any concept at any level of abstraction can be captured in a single word, but it does require a shared definition between the writer and the reader if there is to be shared meaning, because the actual visual form of the word is arbitrary.

Returning to the diagonal axis, it is our experience that there is often tension between the different communities that create and use the models, who tend to lie at opposite ends of the Continuum, as illustrated in Figure 2.8.

Anyone who has worked on transformation programmes will recognise the tendency for two cultures to form around (1) the people and change community, who are trying to create shared meaning and motivation for change across a disparate group of stakeholders, and (2) the technical implementation community who are trying to figure out in enough technical detail what the future state will look like, in order to bring it about.

Depending on your context you may know these communities under different names, and they may not divide into two groups as cleanly as this; what's important is not the exact names or boundaries but the recognition that something is driving the different groups at each end of the Continuum to model change in very different ways. In a programme context, the people and change community will tend to work with free-form presentation diagrams, metaphorical rich pictures, cartoon-like user journeys, videos, design-led prototypes and the like. Systems engineers

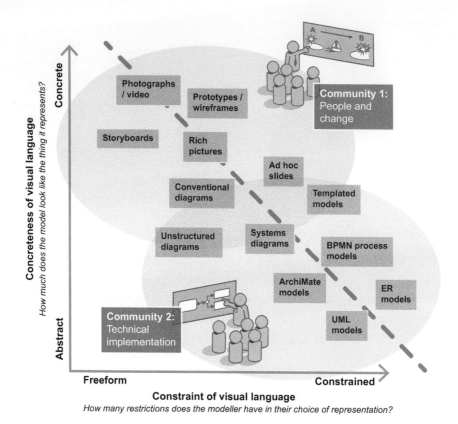

Figure 2.8 The Visualisation Continuum and associated communities

will probably be using standards-driven modelling languages, either domain-specific or generic like UML, in order to ensure that the meaning is more tightly circumscribed. Many change consultants do not know what UML is, let alone how to read a UML diagram. All too often technical engineers won't even look at rich pictures because their meaning is not clearly enough defined. Community 1 has a tendency to look down on community 2 as being 'in the weeds', too obsessed with precision and detail, unable to see the big picture, while community 2 tends to look down on community 1 as having their heads in the clouds, creating 'pretty pictures', unclear about what they mean, blind to the technical limitations of the path they are pursuing. And so the two communities become disconnected.

There are groups within each community trying to bridge the chasm (think Design Thinking in community 1 or TOGAF[12] in community 2, for example), but in our view none of these groups have sufficiently grasped the extent to which the problem is one of representation and meaning. An architectural model built using TOGAF, for example, can connect the capability of an individual IT platform, through a series of associations (of other capabilities), to the top-level mission of the organisation. In theory, management should be poring over the model to understand the consequences and constraints of transformation decisions; the reason they don't is not because it isn't accurate or useful, but because they can't read it!

Yet the fact that these two communities have different visualisation needs, and produce artefacts that look very different, only masks the fact that they are *fundamentally talking about the same things*.

One of the key purposes of this book is to encourage members of each of these communities to appreciate the work and outputs of the other, and to pursue ways of integrating them together more tightly. A pictorial vision that everyone can understand and buy into is useless if no one knows how to implement it. A model that perfectly expresses how to implement a change is useless if no one understands it. We need to find better ways of achieving both at the same time.

Notes

1 Gantt charts are examples of models of the transformation itself, but they model the activities of the delivery team doing the transformation, not the organisation that is being transformed.
2 Jackson, M. (2003). *Systems Thinking: Creative Holism for Managers*. Chichester: John Wiley & Sons.
3 Ackoff, R. (1981). *Creating the Corporate Future*. New York: John Wiley & Sons.
4 Morris, C. (1964). *Signification and Significance*. Cambridge: MIT Press.
5 www.iiba.org/babok-guide.aspx, accessed July 29, 2019.
6 http://sebokwiki.org/wiki/Types_of_Models, accessed July 29, 2019.
7 Business Process Model and Notation; see www.bpmn.org/, accessed July 29, 2019.
8 The Unified Modeling Language; see www.uml.org/, accessed July 29, 2019.
9 The Systems Modeling Language; see www.omgsysml.org/, accessed July 29, 2019.

10 The ArchiMate® Enterprise Architecture Modeling Language; see www.open group.org/archimate-forum/archimate-overview, accessed July 29, 2019.
11 Oblique Strategies is a set of cards originally developed by Brian Eno and Peter Schmidt in the 1970s to help artists overcome creative blocks; each card contains a pithy statement or question (e.g. 'Use an old idea', 'What would your closest friend do?') intended to stimulate lateral thinking.
12 The Open Group Architecture Framework; see www.opengroup.org/togaf, accessed July 29, 2019.

The transformation journey

The approach to change

Change paradigms

We ended the previous chapter by dividing the world of organisational change into two communities, a divide that most people with any substantial experience of transformation programmes will recognise. So, where does it come from? This is a book about visual models, not a book about organisational theory, but this is still a hugely important question; people's presuppositions about what organisations are and how they change has a huge impact on the kinds of models they see as being valuable or even valid. We will call these sets of basic presuppositions 'paradigms'. Paradigms are the 'habitats' in which different kinds of visual model live, the worldviews in which they make sense. When someone judges the value of a particular visual model, it's important to be able to understand the paradigm in which it is being judged, in order to put the praise and/or criticism in context.

The two paradigms that are most significant for our purposes are what we will call for now the 'mechanistic' and the 'organic'. These, or related metaphors, tend to be the first two on academic lists of organisational paradigms (e.g. Morgan 1997,[1] Smith and Graetz 2011[2]), and their assumptions permeate the language of change, for example:

- **Mechanistic language**: 'What *levers* can we apply?', 'How do we *upgrade* this capability?', 'How do we *re-engineer* our processes?', 'How do we *fix* our operations?', 'Is this function *performing* adequately?';

- **Organic language**: 'How do we *adapt* to the changing customer need?', 'How do we *spawn* new ideas more rapidly?', 'How do we *mature* our service offerings?', 'How can we *grow* as an organisation?', 'Do we have resilience *in our DNA*?', 'When will the change *take root*?'.

If you instinctively see organisations in a more mechanical way, then you are likely to see change as an engineering process – upgrading or transforming the mechanism so that it can deliver a new capability. Your language becomes one of designing the solution, creating blueprints, delivering capabilities, optimising performance. The defining feature of this paradigm, in our context, is that it tends to see change as **deterministic**. You can *determine* what needs to happen, *determine* the plan to make it happen, and deliver on the plan to achieve *pre-determined* results. This is only possible when you conceive of the organisation as something that functions in a pre-determined way, like a machine.

If you instinctively see organisations in a more organic or biological way, then you are more likely to see change as an adaptive process – so you might talk about helping the business to learn, respond and mature. The defining feature of this paradigm is that it sees change as **emergent**. Changes in the organisation's environment *emerge* over time, and the correct response needs to *emerge* through iterative experiment and adaptation. You cannot pre-determine how an organisation will respond to a change in its environment, let alone a change that you try to instigate on its behalf.

Although we don't have space to discuss the point in more detail, we would argue that most of the other philosophies and metaphors that could be listed,[3] or at least the mental models that they inhabit, tend towards one or other of these two extremes.

The determinist and emergent paradigms in model-making

As illustrated in Figure 3.1, the continuum between these extremes map onto our earlier continuum of visual models. Those in the bottom right tend to see the world in a more mechanistic/deterministic way and therefore tend to favour diagrams that show precision and exactitude, as these will be most helpful when trying to 'upgrade' the organisation. Those in the top left tend to favour models that are easy to understand, because they want to inspire a co-ordinated response from the organisation as a living system. This is, of course, a huge generalisation – there are plenty of change managers and designers who are very comfortable working in a mechanistic mindset when

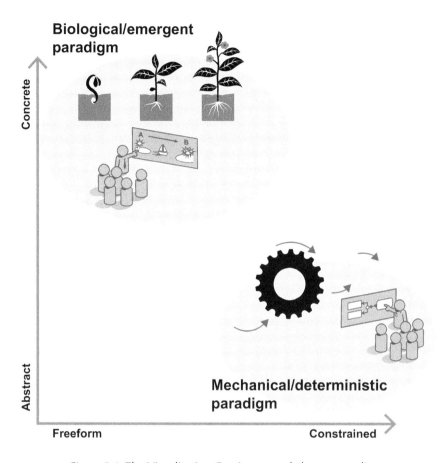

Figure 3.1 The Visualisation Continuum and change paradigms

the problem at hand can be straightforwardly codified and solved using best practice, and there are plenty of programme managers and business architects who can work in an emergent, organic way when the situation is equivocal and requires imagination and active experimentation. This kind of mental ambidexterity is a species of what Dave Gray has called 'liminal thinking'; 'liminal' is Latin for 'threshold', so liminal thinking is that which exists on the threshold between different domains.

> The idea behind liminal thinking is that there are thresholds, doors of opportunity, around you, all the time. Most of them are invisible to you, because you are focusing on other things. But they are there, they are

real, and they offer incredible potential for growth and change. Tuning your mind to liminal thinking will help you *see* opportunities that others will be unable to *see* or even imagine. It's a kind of psychological agility that enables you to create change where others cannot.[4]

The ability to think in this way is, in our experience, not very common, but it's certainly one that can be learned and developed. Notice the emphasis on seeing in that quote: 'Liminal thinking will help you *see* opportunities that others will be unable to *see* or even imagine.'

In this chapter, we want to start that journey by looking at how people's different ways of thinking play out in the visuals they prefer to create and the visuals they see as being useful. During the process we will move through three sets of common approaches to change, and look at the kind of diagrams used in each. We will take the Programme-led approach as an archetype of the mechanistic paradigm, the Design-led approach as an archetype of the emergent paradigm, and Systems-led approaches as examples of the space in between. Most large-scale organisational changes will involve a combination of these approaches (although they will usually be under the umbrella of a programme for the purposes of governance and funding).

If nothing else, we hope to demonstrate that no paradigm is right or wrong, just as no particular methodology is right or wrong. We are more likely to achieve the desired change when we are willing to see the world through other people's eyes, and we are willing to adapt our approach to the circumstances. But until we are aware of our own biases and presuppositions, we will not be open to seeing the value in these other perspectives.

Programmes: upgrading the machine

The dominant approach to large-scale change in organisations remains Programme Management,[5] an approach that we see as being rooted firmly in the deterministic paradigm. This reflects the fact that, despite a marked shift in recent decades, the machine metaphor is still the overwhelmingly dominant way that most people think and talk in large organisations, even those who want to see them in a more organic and human light. The language is so engrained that most of us don't even notice it. We call organisational units 'functions', not 'organs'. 'Functions' are made up of 'processes', not 'cells'. So, when we want to change, we need to define the change in advance and create a programme to 'deliver' it for us.

To illustrate, look at the process for Programme Management as defined in the UK Government's Managing Successful Programmes (MSP) framework, which we have illustrated in Figure 3.2. MSP describes a programme as something that will 'deliver a coherent organizational capability that is released into operational use according to a schedule that delivers maximum incremental improvements with minimal adverse operational impact'.[6] This diagram is not part of the specification, but it illustrates the

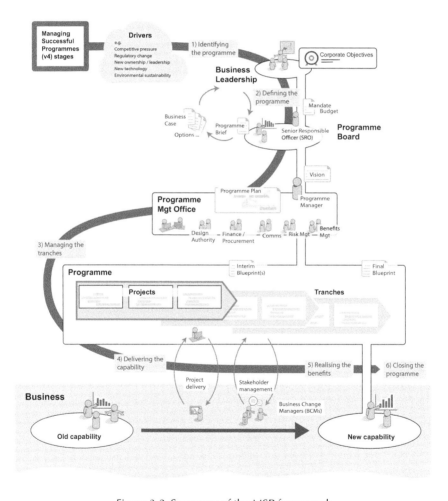

Figure 3.2 Summary of the MSP framework

stages defined by the specification mapped onto a typical programme structure. The 'delivery of the capability' is at the bottom, and the rest of the diagram reflects what's implicit in the framework and near-ubiquitous in practice – that change is a top-down process, where the new capability requirements are determined at a senior level by the management team, and delivered as a kind of 'upgrade' to the organisation.

You might dispute that MSP has these ideological commitments built into it – could this not be seen as simply a neutral framework for a programme, which could be delivered under any paradigm? No! Even the underlying metaphor of 'delivering' a programme says something about the mindset. If the change were emergent, then by definition you wouldn't know what it was going to be in advance. In a programme setting, change is reified as a 'thing' that is delivered, a metaphor that only makes sense if you have decided in advance what that thing is, as you can't deliver something that hasn't been defined.

This is not to say that the more people-focused aspects of transformation will necessarily be ignored. All modern transformation programmes will have a budget set aside for people and change activities. In practice this budget is often restricted to training and communication activities, and even if a broader attempt is made at real engagement (where affected stakeholders can actually influence the implementation), even these activities are seen as something that is 'delivered' by business change managers. Engagement is another workstream among many, a set of activities to be delivered, regardless of how much the people in that workstream protest that change cannot be reduced to a mechanistic process.

The products produced during a transformation are often mandated within an organisation's change methodology, which themselves may be derived from industry standards. The MSP standard, for example, proposes the creation of a 'Blueprint' to define what the future state will look like, what the intermediate states will be, and what the current state is. The Blueprint is developed in parallel with the business case and benefit profiles, and is used to determine the projects within the programme that are required to create and deploy the future state; it is an essential deliverable of the programme and one which will almost always include some form of model.

The problem is that although methodologies may specify the products to be created (such as a 'Blueprint' for the future), they don't specify what those products should look like, so the models embedded within them can look quite different even within the same organisation. Adopting standard viewpoints and model standards (as discussed in Chapter 7) can help to improve consistency, assuming that the target audiences are also familiar with those viewpoints and standards.

When change is something that is 'delivered', the visual models that support it are primarily going to be about specifying the change and communicating it to stakeholders. If you see an organisation as an entirely deterministic machine, then after a while the people in it become cogs occupying various positions in the processes that make up the target operating model. The target operating model is the blueprint for the organisational design, just as an engineering schematic is the blueprint for a machine. It may need to be depicted in a pictorial way (like an engagement rich picture), but in a mechanistic paradigm this is a bit like oiling the wheels of the machine – the engineer recognises that entropy exists and does their best to mitigate against it. Pejoratively, the perception becomes that although people exist in the organisation, they don't understand engineering and architectural concepts, so need to have things explained using 'pretty pictures'. This may be exaggerating for effect, but the effect is to illustrate the tendency of the mechanistic paradigm. And regardless of the good intentions of those who lead them, this still remains the underlying philosophy in the vast majority of large-scale transformation programmes. It dominates the language and budget, and it's the backdrop against which people with a more organic perspective have to work.

We are painting an extreme portrait here in order to highlight the underlying paradigm. Clearly, under the Programme umbrella there will be a much broader blend of approaches and philosophies. Many projects under a programme do not know what they are going to achieve before they start, and only make progress through experiment and iteration. The 'waterfall' approach to project delivery has now gone out of fashion in favour of Design Thinking, agile development, scrums and the like. But the fact remains that the archetypal programme under which such projects are delivered has to exist beforehand in order for them to have a budget, and for the programme to exist it has to have something pre-determined to deliver, or else the business case will not be signed off. And as far as the programme is concerned, no matter how emergent the approach taken by an individual project, it is still just a line on a roadmap, fitting into

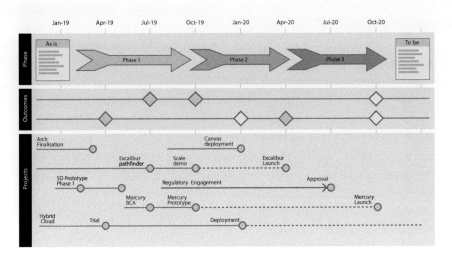

Figure 3.3 A typical transformation programme roadmap

a broader, *pre-determined* sequence of activities, something like the one illustrated in Figure 3.3.

This is the context in which most architectures are first created, in which target operating models are built, in which processes are redefined. The sheer complexity of what is being attempted in a large organisational transformation programme demands a consistency of language and approach, and so the visual models that are created to describe the change tend to be in the bottom right of our Visualisation Continuum: BPMN, UML, SysML and abstract presentation slides.

It's *not* that any of this is wrong – to have any level of control or predictability in large-scale change, it's essential – but it's only one paradigm.

Design Thinking: responding to the environment

For people who instinctively see organisations in a more organic and emergent way, the much-vaunted failure of large-scale programmes is proof that the underlying mechanistic paradigm is wrong. A popular illustration of the difference comes from an example originally used by Richard Dawkins[7] to contrast living and non-living entities: the deterministic paradigm treats change programmes as throwing a stone, where we assume that the destination, trajectory and force can be calculated, so an appropriate programme plan will 'deliver' the correct result. The emergent paradigm sees it as throwing a bird – an organisation, like a bird, is a complex adaptive system, so if all you do is throw it then you can't predict where it's going to end up. It will probably fly off to the nearest tree.

If organisations are more like organisms, then their survival depends not so much on how well someone engineers them, but on how rapidly and successfully they can adapt to changes in their environment. The current shift happening in large organisations away from large-scale programmes and towards design-based innovation is an indication that organisational paradigms are slowly starting to shift.

A good example of this is the huge rise in popularity of the various 'Design Thinking' processes over the last decade. Different authors promote different models and definitions for Design Thinking, but what they all have in common is a *human-centred* approach to solving problems. The Stanford school[8] process shown in Figure 3.4 is probably one of the most familiar, but they are all variations on the same theme.

They start by studying the customer or service user and defining the change requirement according to *their* needs, not according to the expectations of the group doing the study, let alone the organisation's long-term strategy or capability. The problem definition, ideation, prototyping and testing of the solution are done with and for the end user. This has always been the approach of effective designers, but calling it 'Design Thinking' and defining a simple process has allowed the mindset to break out of the confines of what has typically been considered 'design' (product design, graphic design, etc.) and be applied to literally anything – services, business processes, user experiences.

Design Thinking epitomises the emergent paradigm. It actively discourages pre-guessing the user's needs. If the customer base is the environment and the organisation is the organism that lives in that environment, Design Thinking is

Figure 3.4 A typical Design Thinking process

encouraging the organism to become much more tightly coupled to its environment, so that it can respond more flexibly to observed reality, not some hypothetical strategic conjecture. The big difference between this approach and the Programmatic approach is that we genuinely don't know in advance what the solution will be. Indeed, we don't even know what the problem will be! This becomes obvious when we try to illustrate the process as a shift of capability, as we did before for Programme Management. Whereas we could illustrate the entire MSP process with no reference to end users at all, this is impossible for Design Thinking. Figure 3.5 attempts to show the Design Thinking steps from Figure 3.2 overlaid onto the capability delivery associated with Programme Management – it is obvious that the iterative, emergent approach of one does not mesh easily with the linear, single-timeframe approach of the other.

This change in emphasis brings a huge shift in the style and rationale of visual models created, in that they are built organically, iteratively and responsively to the emerging understanding of the situation. Typically, the approach is delivered through creative, hands-on workshops involving physical modelling materials, Post-it notes, huge sheets of paper, white-boards and so on, with the prospective customer or user at the centre of the process. For many people on the more structured, programme-oriented end of change, the outputs of these workshops don't deserve to be called models, as they are too organic and under-specified.

But clustering Post-it notes around themes and perspectives is a way of aligning the mental models of participants – captured in Figure 3.6. Each

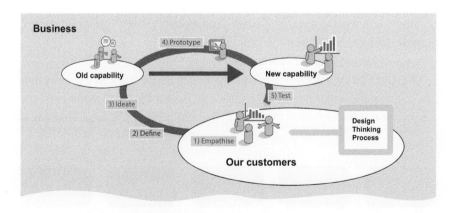

Figure 3.5 Design Thinking and the emergent change process

Figure 3.6 A Design Thinking workshop
Reproduced under licence.[9]

Post-it is an 'atom' of meaning, looking for a place in a larger structure. What we see in these workshops is an emergent model, co-created by the group, built around the needs of the user, slowly coming into being. In the earlier stages of change, when the solution is not known, this kind of flexibility is essential.

The hype around Design Thinking has elevated it almost to a religion in certain quarters. It's easy to understand and it makes sense. While the obvious application is to the world of innovation and start-ups, it's so general that it feels like it can be applied to any problem in any context. In our experience this is simply not the case, for one simple reason: most organisations are not starting from a blank sheet of paper. All too often, when undertaken in large, established businesses, Design Thinking work-shops generate a huge level of energy among participants, several fascinating ideas, and then an equivalent level of disappointment as so few of the ideas come to fruition. Putting the organic paradigm together with our general principle that models stand for things more complex than themselves, we get another way to understand what is happening: the work-shops are destroying a huge amount of complexity about the environment and generating insights about users and potential solutions that are refreshingly simple and clear, as captured by Daniel Newman's popular 'design squiggle'[10] illustration, shown in Figure 3.7.

Noise / Uncertainty / Patterns / Insights   Clarity / Focus

Research & Synthesis   Concept / Prototype   Design

Figure 3.7 The design squiggle
Reproduced under licence.[11]

The trouble is that they tend not to destroy an equivalent amount of complexity about the organisation in which they are run. This makes them perfect for start-ups and innovation labs, in which there is no parent organisation, no existing IT, no existing customer contracts, no legacy processes. When all these things exist, the squiggle of design above reaches the point of 'scale' and instead of flat-lining into something simple and clear, meets a far more intimidating mess of existing priorities, processes, structures and people coming from the other direction. This is the challenge that large companies are currently facing in the race for 'digitisation'. They are competing against digital start-ups who are not hampered by legacy structure. Thinking in terms of the organic paradigm, the emphasis is all on the environment, and not on the organism that needs to adapt to that environment. Any large-scale transformation has to find a way to address both at the same time. How? Enter the systems paradigm.

Systemic approaches

Although the hype that used to exist around systems theories and cybernetics in the second half of the twentieth century has been dwarfed by the hype around Design Thinking in the early twenty-first century, there is a rich intellectual tradition to tap into that is slowly being rediscovered. The systems tradition covers a very broad range of practices, which span the spectrum from the deterministic paradigm (mathematical approaches like Operations Research, Systems Dynamics, Control Theory) to the emergent paradigm (e.g. Soft Systems Methodology, Critical Systems Heuristics, Complexity approaches). However, all of these traditions share the same simple observation that complex socio-technical systems (like work organisations) reflect the behaviour of living systems in responding adaptively to their environment. In this way, they differ from Design Thinking in that they have a balanced view, not just of the complexity of the environment but of the system that exists in that environment.

We will spend more time discussing the different kinds of freeform models used in both Systems and Design Thinking approaches in Chapter 6, but here we will look at just one form of model to illustrate the systems paradigm, which is the Viable System Model (VSM) of Stafford Beer.[12] The VSM is an idealised model of the structure required for any system to continue to exist in a changing environment. On the one hand, VSM seems firmly in the organic paradigm – the original template for the model was the human nervous system, as the most sophisticated example we have in nature of a self-sustaining system (see Figure 3.8). On the other hand, Beer works out the detail of the model as a series of complexity equations, expressed in the engineering language of variety 'attenuation' and 'amplification'.

Although Beer's works on VSM are not easy-going, the basic structure of five interconnected subsystems is straightforward, and practitioners will talk about 'doing a quick VSM' to sketch out the underlying dynamics of the system in question. Each line in the diagram represents a feedback loop where, for the system to be healthy, each element can manage the complexity generated by the elements it is connected to.

Which paradigm is this? Using the model for organisation design feels deterministic – we are specifying how things should be – yet the whole premise of the model is based on the probabilistic ways that organisms respond to environmental uncertainty. The Viable System Model, relatively unknown outside the field of systems theory and cybernetics, perfectly illustrates how systemic approaches bridge the divide between the paradigms.

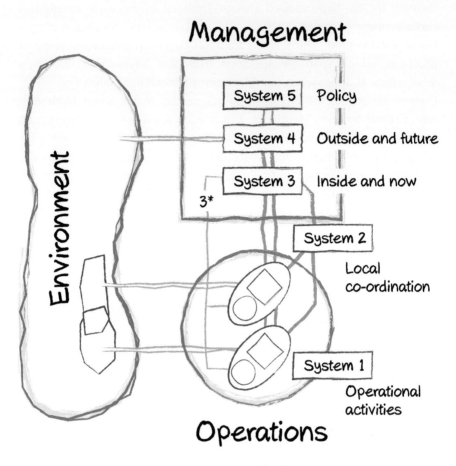

Figure 3.8 A VSM sketch

Developing a portfolio of paradigms

Paradigms are really just mental models. They are sets of assumptions that we don't notice, but which underpin the models we make and the value we see in those models. Even when things don't go right, our tendency is still to hold onto our paradigms and blame the people who don't see it our way for why it's gone wrong. Our argument here is not that one or other paradigm is correct and others are wrong, but that the more we learn to recognise them in ourselves and others, the broader a repertoire we are going to be able to deploy – both as individuals and as teams – to meet the needs of the situation.

44

So, in a complex, highly ambiguous situation, for example, stepping into a more emergent paradigm is likely to see us creating more freeform models involving a wider range of stakeholders, asking more open questions and using live diagramming techniques to try to find a way to understand the problem. Immediately setting up a programme team with structures to deliver a solution is probably not the best way forward when we don't even know what the problem is. But if we do know the problem and the solution is already at hand (an incremental IT upgrade, say), we won't get very far if no one is willing to step into a deterministic paradigm and start putting together the solution architecture and project plan.

On the vast majority of transformations, the crucial thing is not to pick a paradigm but to be able to gather an appropriate blend from across the whole spectrum. Most transformation starts with a high degree of uncertainty, in which a Design Thinking or systems inquiry approach is likely to be most appropriate, involving rich pictures, user stories, causal loop diagrams and so on. As the change progresses, activity will need to be programmed that affects the existing estate, which will need to be modelled mechanistically. If the ongoing engagement of staff follows this mechanistic approach though, it's more likely to alienate than inspire people, as they feel they are being 'done unto' by the programme.

Where to next?

Visual models are windows into the paradigms of the people who create them. If we want to harness the diversity of paradigms that exist across our transformation team, if we want to engage with the variety of perspectives of those affected by the change, if we want to enlarge our own worldviews and find shared meaning with other people, then it's worthwhile investing time developing a greater appreciation for modelling techniques we are unfamiliar with. The next part of the book takes us on a tour of these techniques, from the top left of the Visualisation Continuum to the bottom right.

In the world of development and philanthropy, proposals for investment in social change initiatives are commonly accompanied by what is called a 'Theory of Change', a model that provides the rationale for why a particular investment will lead, through a sequence of subordinate outcomes, to the overall outcome for the system in question. What we have been claiming through this chapter is that there are in effect higher level, paradigmatic 'theories of change' that are often presupposed or go unspoken. It is often these paradigms, rather than the models they generate, that are in conflict with one another. Therefore, as we progress through the various examples, be aware of how you respond emotionally as well as intellectually to each, and reflect on what this says about your own underlying 'theory of change', and the prejudices you may hold towards other people's. By the time we reach the final part of the book we will, hopefully, be in a better position to make meaningful proposals for how to draw the different paradigms together.

Notes

1 Morgan, G. (2006). *Images of Organization*. Thousand Oaks, CA: SAGE Publications, Inc.
2 Smith, Aaron C. T. and Graetz, F. M. (2011). *Philosophies of Organizational Change*. Cheltenham: Edward Elgar Publishing.
3 The most influential being Morgan (2006), who gives six other metaphors: brains, cultures, political systems, psychic prisons, flux and transformation, instruments of domination.
4 Gray, D. (2006). *Liminal Thinking*. New York: Two Waves, p. xxii.
5 What we say here about programmes can be equally applied on a larger scale to portfolios of programmes and on a smaller scale to individual projects.
6 Sowden, R., Leigh, G., Mayfield, P. and Venning, C. (2011). *Managing Successful Programmes*. 4th ed. London: Stationery Office Books, p. 21.
7 Dawkins, R. (2006). *The Blind Watchmaker*. Reprint ed. London: Penguin Books.
8 https://dschool.stanford.edu/, accessed July 29, 2019.
9 Photo by @youxventures on www.unsplash.com, accessed July 29, 2019.
10 https://thedesignsquiggle.com/, accessed July 29, 2019.
11 The Process of Design Squiggle by Damien Newman, thedesignsquiggle.com. Shared under CC Attribution-NoDerivs 3.0 United States, https://creativecom mons.org/licenses/by-nd/3.0/us/, accessed July 29, 2019.
12 Beer, S. (1981). *Brain of the Firm*. 2nd ed. Chichester: John Wiley; Beer, S. (1979). *Heart of Enterprise*. Chichester: John Wiley.

A journey along the Visualisation Continuum

Pictures

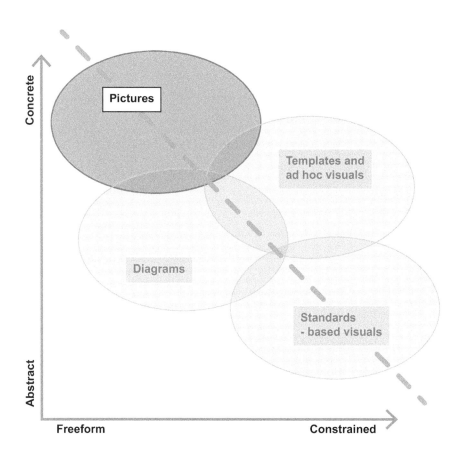

We start our tour of change visuals with pictorial representations, where the appearance of the model is intended to either directly or metaphorically reflect the appearance of the subject. These visuals are generally not entirely pictorial, but rather accompanied by text, although exactly how much text is appropriate or desirable can be a point of contention. Pictorial models tend to be used in two ways:

1   At the start of the change journey, to help support exploratory dialogue, whether that be among business leaders exploring strategic options, or stakeholders exploring problems, needs and desires. These pictures, or more precisely the dialogues they enable, are catalysts for initiating change;
2   During the change journey, to make the rationale and objectives of the transformation more intelligible to a broader range of stakeholders, with a view to gaining buy-in, information and feedback. The typical example of this is in employee engagement activities.

This twofold purpose is perfectly illustrated through the story of 'rich pictures'.

Rich pictures

The idea of a 'rich picture' is now well established in conventional management practice, although there is no single agreed definition of the term. The approach was first made popular through the Soft Systems Methodology (SSM) developed by Peter Checkland and his colleagues at Lancaster University during the 1970s. In our experience, the vast majority of people who use the term 'rich picture' and even those who promote it as an approach have little or no knowledge of SSM. For many change managers, a 'rich picture' is simply a 'picture'. Berg[1] has convincingly demonstrated that there is also no single agreed definition among academics.

In SSM, rich picture exercises are primarily run as sense-making sessions. Typically, participants will draw freeform images, either individually or in groups, of a problematic situation, and then use these depictions to explore the dynamics of the system that are giving rise to those problems. Participants are not constrained in how they visually express themselves, and are actively encouraged to make their depictions as pictorial as possible. A typical example is shown in Figure 4.1.

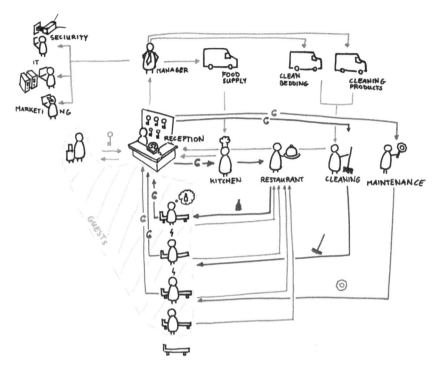

Figure 4.1 A typical SSM rich picture

Although the term 'rich picture' has made it through to mainstream management language, this original association with sense-making work-shops has not. The term is as often used now on transformation pro-grammes to refer to carefully designed, studio-produced depictions of the current and/or future state, used for communication and stakeholder engagement, like the example in Figure 4.2.

Also, consultancies and agencies have sought to differentiate their own visual offerings by giving their pictures a brand name: Learning Maps, Big Pictures, Root Maps, Xplanations, Story Maps and so on. One event that significantly boosted awareness of pictorial approaches to change was the publication in 1998 of a case study in *Harvard Business Review*[2] of the turnaround in fortunes at Sears. The article placed at the centre of this success the approach to employee engagement built around Root's Learn-ing Maps.

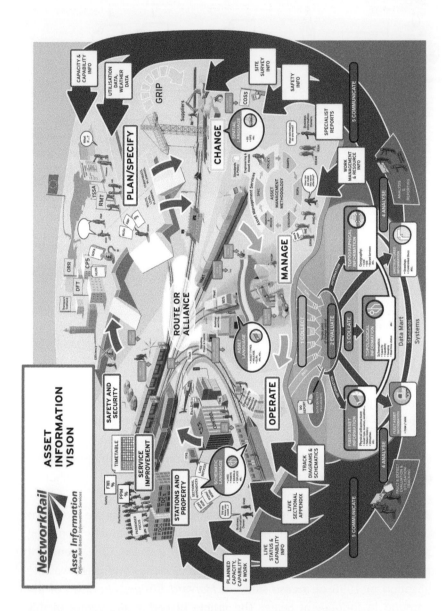

Figure 4.2 A studio-finish rich picture

For illustrative purposes only. Reproduced with permission from Network Rail.

It is now common to call images like this one a 'rich picture', despite them being the opposite of the original SSM approach in having a high level of finish, resulting from multiple iterations with multiple stakeholders, and mapping out a transformation journey rather than the dynamics of a system. 'Rich picture' has now become a standard term for describing all depictions of this kind, regardless of the level of finish, subject matter, source of content or application. While purists might insist that the term should be reserved and only applied to the original SSM approach or approaches consistent with it, it seems unlikely to us that the tide of everyday usage is going to turn anytime soon.

Regardless of how this nomenclature evolves in the future, we believe it is very important to discriminate between the two modes in which rich pictures tend to be used, i.e. sense-making and engagement. Before examining each of these applications, let's summarise the advantages of pictures that are common to both.

Advantages of rich pictures in general

The defining feature of rich pictures is not so much that they are pictorial, but that they attempt to illustrate all of the most relevant factors of a situation *on a single page*, encouraging a higher level, more systemic perspective.

As one lays out the elements of a situation alongside each other, the relationships between them become more salient, which helps to mitigate against silo mentality. If participants in a session all come from different departments but can all see themselves in the picture, the picture becomes a shared perspective through which they can engage in discussion about what's going on *between* departments, which is often where the significant tensions lie.

A good picture can then build shared meaning around this broader perspective, because it is expressed pictorially rather than verbally. This is because common, abstract business words – 'service', 'value', 'capability' and so on – have a myriad of meanings to different people. When the word is accompanied by a picture representing what it means in that context, misinterpretations become harder to make and easier to spot. The process of creating the picture amounts to a group of people asking themselves 'what does this actually look like?' When the question is honestly asked and honestly answered, the resulting pictures can go a long way to creating a shared mental model about what's going on.

Rich pictures as sense-making tools

The use of rich pictures in participatory workshops usually occurs towards the beginning of a transformation journey, as a way of inquiring into the dynamics of the situation.

In a typical session, participants will be given introductory guidelines that boundary the system or problem being explored, and either individually or as a group construct a picture of what is going on from their point of view. There are no defined guidelines for how this should happen, and different practitioners favour different approaches. Groups may each be given the same or different questions or perspectives to explore, may or may not be given support materials to get started (e.g. a set of pre-drawn icons or images of common concepts), and may or may not combine their insights and images into richer pictures that integrate the different perspectives later in the workshop. In all cases though, the primary role of the pictures is to stimulate dialogue both during and subsequent to the session, from which insights can be gained to inform potential solutions.

There are many advantages to using rich pictures in this way in addition to the general ones described above. The most obvious is that the pictures are the participants' own creations. They are not mediated by a professional artist or a consultant telling them what to draw, so are much more likely to arouse genuine empathy in the group. Listening to people describe their own drawings frequently creates 'aha' moments as listeners understand for the first time what it's like to see the world from that person's point of view. Strength of feeling often shines through much more strongly in people's drawings than it does in their words. Patterns in thinking between each individual or group become strikingly obvious when they are laid out visually.

One might complain that the lack of visual language skills is an impediment to shared meaning: might non-artists continually misinterpret one another's work? This criticism only makes sense when the pictures are divorced from the dialogical context of the workshops, in which it is often creative 'accidents' and misinterpretations that lead to the most interesting questions and insights in the conversation ('You saw the picture like that? Wow – we would never have seen that!'). If the session is aiming to generate an engagement tool as described below, then the addition of a professional artist to the process makes sense, but experience suggests that in a sense-making context it can be much harder to engage with a picture created by a third party in quite the same way as that created by the group itself. Even though the artist may be listening intently and accurately reflecting the discussion, they themselves do not play a direct part in the system they are depicting, and so will always create a different kind of energy. When a group is generating a picture of a world that they themselves inhabit, the creation process informs the discussion, which in turn informs the creation and so on. The picture takes on a life of its own, and results in an artefact that the group is invested in because they themselves directly created it.

How should rich picture sense-making sessions be best run in practice? Bell, Berg and Morse[3] detail some basic guidelines from their experience, summarised as follows:

- Groups of four, five or six participants;
- Groups, where possible, should be in 'cabaret style' seating (i.e. small tables scattered around a large room);
- Paper should be flipchart size;
- At least four coloured pens per table (black, blue, red and green as a minimum);
- At least 40 minutes allowed for drawing;
- Put some chairs around the room to allow the facilitator to watch and listen at a reasonable distance;
- There is no need for participants to be seated whilst drawing;
- Do not encourage eating and drinking whilst picturing;
- You can audio- and videotape the session but be aware of permissions and the possible negative effect this type of intrusion might have on your group.

Clearly, the other major consideration affecting the quality of outcome is the quality of facilitation. Besides the general qualities required of any good facilitator (in terms of attitude, manner, voice, level of intervention, etc.), rich pictures add a significant additional challenge, which is that of getting people to participate in the first place. Bell et al. describe it thus:

The biggest problem for a facilitator is to convince adults that drawing pictures is a valuable exercise. If you announce what you are going to be doing in your workshop beforehand there is a good chance people might not even bother to show ...

We are very schooled to notions of 'value-for-money', 'best practice', 'impact', 'quantifiable outcomes', 'evidence-based practice' and drawing pictures over a longish period just cuts across so much of our contemporary culture of accountability and assessment. "What purposeful and accountable activity did you do today?" "I drew pictures with my colleagues!"[4]

They go on to suggest some practical ways to overcome this difficulty:

- Explain the rationale for using pictures at the outset, emphasising the ability of pictures throughout human history to transcend cultural, educational and language barriers;
- Show rather than tell, e.g. take an extract of a picture from a previous session and ask the group how they would articulate the meaning of the image purely in words;
- Demonstrate the picture superiority effect (by sharing some of the evidence that information is better retained when accompanied by relevant pictures);
- Emphasise that there is no expectation regarding the artistic skill of the participants – you are interested in meaning, not aesthetics.

Rich pictures as engagement tools

For many readers the use of rich pictures as an SSM-based discovery/ sense-making tool as described above will be novel, even though this is the original derivation of the term. We suspect the main reason for this is simple arithmetic: many more people have attended rich picture-based whole-organisation engagement sessions than could ever attend a series of small-group discovery sessions, and so the rich picture has come to be known as an employee engagement tool. How does it work?

Typically, leaders and key stakeholders are invited to a combination of individual and group workshops to gather together the content for the picture, which is normally produced by a third party. After a series of iterative drafts and workshops, the picture is signed off. Even if they facilitate the workshops themselves, most teams will at least feel the need for professional artistic support to produce the final artwork. Many artists who provide live artwork services to group workshops (see below) now also sell 'rich picture' services to meet this need.

Once pictures are completed, they get used in all sorts of ways, ranging from the highly interactive (facilitated small-group discussion sessions involving the whole workforce) to the highly un-interactive (posters and screen-savers). The devolution of the term 'rich picture' from its original use to describe an inquiry process into soft systems to its current use to describe artwork printed on mugs and mouse mats is – in our opinion – somewhat depressing. These are completely different things that both just happen to use pictorial representations. There is a place for visualisations of key strategic concepts to be displayed consistently and ubiquitously – much as internal brand messages are deployed by internal marketing and communications departments. But this type of top-down communication is a different need, one for which a complex picture on its own is rarely the solution. Much of the negative reaction to the term 'rich pictures' over the years has arisen from complex, ambiguous artwork being pushed out through every available channel without any context, story or opportunity for discussion. The irony is that for many of the communications teams pushing out the content, the reason for turning to pictures is a desire to increase the level of 'employee engagement', but the pictures end up having the opposite effect. Employee engagement was defined in a 2009 UK government report[5] as:

> A workplace approach designed to ensure that employees are committed to their organization's goals and values, motivated to contribute to organizational success, and are able at the same time to enhance their own sense of well-being.[6]

The need for this approach is never more pronounced than during times of change. The authors go on to highlight the fact that:

> In particular, engagement is two way: organizations must work to engage the employee, who in turn has a choice about the level of engagement to offer the employer. Each reinforces the other.[7]

This is the gold standard for an employee engagement rich picture intervention. Does the employee feel that the process is genuinely two-way?

The authors of the report propose four 'enablers' of engagement, which are helpful benchmarks to use when planning a rich picture rollout:

1 *Strategic narrative* – will the picture provide a strong story of where the organisation has come from and where it's going, which is clearly owned and articulated by the leadership?
2 *Engaging managers* – will line managers have the capacity to facilitate honest dialogue when using the picture, dialogue that respects and treats people as individuals with their own ideas and opinions?
3 *Employee voice* – will people feel that they are genuinely being involved in the change, so that the ideas and opinions they express in response to the picture will make a difference to how the change is implemented?
4 *Integrity* – will the promises and the intent inherent in the picture play out in the reality that the employees go on to experience?

There are no accepted standards for what a picture designed for engagement ought to look like. The challenge is to combine a large amount of abstract and often equivocal content into a form that is clear and easy to absorb, and that will not just represent the leadership story but connect to the experience of the people affected. Engaging pictures tend to:

- **Tell a story**: the story is what people will remember and engage with – the picture is there to bring the story of change to life;
- **Have a simple core structure**: it's not just that too much content is hard to understand, it's that it turns people off. If you want to engage a target audience, then tell a simple story clearly, don't distract them with lots of extraneous information;
- **Have enough richness to seem real**: at the same time, a picture that is too simplistic may lack the nuance to reflect the experience of different audience groups. Clever design can allow a huge amount of information to be portrayed without being overwhelming. The key is to use visual language (colour, size, spacing, positioning, etc.) to guide the eye from the most important, central elements to the small vignettes that illustrate the subordinate points. We cover some of these points in Chapter 9;
- **Allow breathing space**: too often managers creating pictures see blank areas as wasteful, and fill them up with content. If there is no space between things on a page then everything becomes part of an undifferentiated mass;

- **Involve employees**: it's important to present early drafts to a wide range of employees to see how they respond, and incorporate their content into the final version. This is a great way of getting historically taboo subjects that have been blocking change discussed in an open forum. If these are part of the picture then it feels 'legitimate' to talk about them with colleagues. This can help break down some of the 'them vs us' sense that tends to accompany transformation;
- **Avoid jargon**: the whole point of the picture is to illustrate what the change will actually look like in practice, which many change leaders find hard. Sometimes nobody really knows what it will look like, so the easy way out is to recycle the jargon of the programme along with meaningless elements of clip art in a metaphorical landscape and call it a rich picture. This approach is more likely to alienate stakeholders than engage them.

Picking up on this last point, the only way to avoid an abstract, meaningless picture is to doggedly and repeatedly ask content holders 'what does that actually look like?' When this is done well, a second benefit emerges, which is an increase in the level of alignment among the leadership. Indeed, many teams that have created rich pictures in the past see this as the primary benefit. Depicting abstract concepts pictorially forces contributors to be clearer about what they actually mean by business jargon. This brings the application of the rich picture closer to its original, exploratory application.

Sense-making vs engagement

Although the extension of the term 'rich picture' beyond the participatory workshop context in recent years is to be welcomed, in that it has brought the advantages of freeform visualisation to a wider audience, there are problems. In sense-making rich picture sessions, the meaning is 'in the room' – people who weren't present in the session are not expected to interpret the artwork in the same way as the people who were. Once the rich picture becomes a communication device however, the meaning 'outside the room' becomes just as important. Too often, rich pictures of visions and end states are created by programme teams and committees behind closed doors, finished by professional studios and sent out to be used for employee engagement, all oblivious of the fact that the picture means so much less to people who weren't involved in its creation.

A good example of this is the overuse of creative metaphors. The development team might come up with an overarching metaphor that makes sense to them in their workshop (e.g. the transformation is a voyage, a race, a building site …), and start to incorporate all the content into that metaphor. So, if the picture is laid out as a motor race, the vision might become the chequered flag, training and development might become the pit stop, and shareholders and customers might become the fans in the grandstand.

This is a very attractive route if you are in the room, because it offers an easy way of breaking down the complexity. In one of our companies, we sometimes use a case study of an onion soup business. Every time we use this in a training context, at least one participant will base their whole picture of the business around the shape of an onion. *If* all of the content fits neatly into an iconic form or a metaphor in this way, then the results can be fantastic, because the metaphor sticks in people's minds and becomes an iconic representation of the transformation.

The trouble is that it's almost never as straightforward as this. Usually there are several aspects of the story or the system that are important but simply don't fit the overarching analogy. If we are on a voyage, then maybe the regulators are the harbour authority, operations are the engine room, marketing are standing on the quayside, but after a while the number of parallels runs out, and participants are trying to label seagulls, buoys, clouds and passing oil tankers in increasingly bizarre ways. It may make perfect sense to the workshop participants creating the picture 'inside the room', but once it goes out as an engagement tool into the organisation people find it patronising or just comical.

A much safer route is to choose a much more generic metaphor – a journey, for example – that can be populated with a series of more conventional representations that everyone will relate to.

Rich pictures and paradigms of change

Rich pictures are a great illustration of how the use of visual tools is shaped by the paradigms we discussed in Chapter 3. What started out as a tool for exploring soft systems (emergent paradigm) became a tool for delivering programmes (deterministic paradigm). This journey is played out every time a rich picture is created as an engagement tool, with the meaning starting out subjective and contingent as workshop participants try to figure out what the programme is doing, and ending up hardened in the output of a single picture designed to send a consistent message to all stakeholders.

Why did this shift happen for rich pictures and not the other varieties of system diagramming techniques we consider now? Surely the reason is simply that the output of a rich picture is so much more concrete than a typical diagram. People like pictures because they can relate to them. Communication managers on programmes commission them because they provoke more interaction with stakeholders than simple top-down messaging, but this probably has more to do with the inherent accessibility of the medium than the systemic nature of the content.

The rich picture story illustrates another phenomenon surrounding the use of visuals in business, which is the difficulty of terminology. In our experience, once we leave the world of standards-based modelling (UML, BPMN, etc.), there are very few diagram types whose definition and characteristics are unambiguously and universally agreed. We will see this even more clearly in Chapter 6, when we look at popular diagramming techniques.

Enter 'visual thinking'

Creating 'rich pictures' offers huge opportunity and huge challenges. Using the full range of possibilities of visual language, rather than just the narrow subset prescribed by a particular diagramming technique or modelling language, gives managers the freedom to present information in a way that resonates more directly with the mental models of their staff; in other words, it increases shared meaning. The challenge is that most managers have limited artistic skills/ambitions, so where do these pictures come from?

Given the mixture of opportunity and challenge, this has become an area ripe for professionalisation. And, indeed, over recent decades this has steadily been happening, under the guise of the 'visual thinking' movement. This is another very loosely defined term, which we will associate with three trends that are rapidly becoming mainstream:

• **Live artworking**: the use of professional illustrators, artists and cartoonists to visually capture the content of workshops and meetings as they proceed;

- **Visual skills development**: upskilling the workforce to think and work in a more visual way;
- **Visual process support tools**: the use of templated visual materials, tools and techniques to support group workshops and meetings.

We look at each of these in turn in the following sections.

Live artworking

There are various names for this practice – 'graphic facilitation', 'graphic recording' and 'scribing' are the most common – and a vibrant and growing ecosystem of practitioners and resources; see the example captured in Figure 4.3.

While some practitioners work solo, the vast majority partner with process consultants and facilitators to deliver visual workshop and meeting experiences. Whilst the practice has only become mainstream in the last decade or so, it has roots in design, consulting and innovation going

Figure 4.3 Live artworking
Reproduced under licence.[8]

back at least 50 years. One of the discipline's leading practitioners, David Sibbet, described his first exposure to graphic recording in a retrospective:

> I first encountered graphic recording of group process in 1972 when the training organization I was working with, the Coro Foundation, moved into a building south of Market Street in San Francisco next to a consulting firm called Interaction Associates (IA). Led by two former architects, David Straus and Michael Doyle, IA was working on a special project called 'Tools for Change' under a grant from the Carnegie Foundation. They were gathering examples of problem solving strategies that teachers could use with students, including ones used by designers and other creative professionals. Active group facilitation was one of the strategies they were very excited about.[9]

Elsewhere Sibbet has described how, when working on Apple's flagship leadership programme in the 1980s, he was 'animated by the idea of building a "graphical user interface" for the workshop that was as accessible and compelling as the one Apple was developing for the computer'.[10] Sibbet's company[11] has been working ever since to bring this vision about through their training, books and resources.

There are now thousands of live artworkers around the world. The vast majority are artists, illustrators and designers (either by training or inclination) who have moved to work in corporate settings, not the other way around. While live artwork is on the whole very much on the emergent side of our spectrum of paradigms, there is variation, which becomes evident from scanning the steady stream of books being published or self-published each year by different practitioners. These authors' descriptions of their work range from being down-to-earth (Brandy Agerback describes her practice of graphic facilitation as 'serving a group by writing and drawing their conversation live and large to help them do their work'[12]) to esoteric (Kelvy Bird describes her practice of 'generative scribing' as offering 'one access route to a sacred way of being, where the spirit of our humanity prevails over any individual agenda'[13]). Whether down-to-earth or esoteric, we are still paradigmatically a long way from a typical systems-engineering- or enterprise-architecture-driven approach.

As visual thinking becomes more mainstream, the distinction between terms is blurring, and it's becoming harder to tell the difference between traditional graphic recording of consultant-led workshops and the kind of service design workshops run by design agencies. The real question is, what difference does it make to include live artworking as part of a meeting, workshop or conference? Live artworking offers many of the advantages we have already met in this chapter – the catalyst for group sense-making, the ability to see the overall flow of the dialogue represented on the wall, the more systemic mode of thought that is encouraged and so on. But given that all of these outcomes can be achieved through good facilitation using the kinds of traditional diagramming techniques we have already encountered, why add a professional artist or cartoonist?

Here's Brandy Agerbeck again:

> I see the power of using drawings as a thinking tool every day of my professional life. I see people light up when they make new connections to their work by looking at my drawings. I see them open up when they see their contribution captured, making them more receptive to other people's ideas.[14]

Diagrams are typically composed of words and lines. When someone actually draws a picture of what people are talking about, rather than just writing it down, and that picture actually resonates with the mental models of the audience, the effect can be electric. This is the aspiration. Talking to a lot of graphic facilitators though, and observing how they are used in practice, it's hard to avoid the conclusion that the appeal is often purely aesthetic on the basis that having something colourful and visual emerging at the side of the room will create a 'halo effect', casting a glow of creativity and dynamism on the rest of the meeting. The artist is hired on a day rate and expected to turn up and 'perform', while being kept (consciously or unconsciously) separate from the design and facilitation of the session. This is probably the number one frustration for live artworkers that we speak to. If one way to assess the value of the artwork created is its ongoing use beyond the meeting itself, then this artwork is of limited value to the organisation.

Where live artworking comes into its own is when the 'performance' aspect is tightly bound to the structure and conduct of the session. This presupposes that:

- The artworker is involved in the preparation and structure of the session;
- The structure of the artwork in some way reflects the structure and purpose of the session;
- The artworker has a level of domain knowledge that allows them to take an active part in the unfolding of the session.

Unless the artist has a reasonable understanding of what is being talked about, there is a danger that what they produce will be more of a detraction than an addition. The difficulty is obviously that the generalist with an illustration background cannot be an expert in all the domains of all their clients. However, this is the challenge that all facilitators and process consultants have to overcome. Another solution, as we will see in the next section, is for those consultants and facilitators to increase their visual thinking abilities for themselves.

Visual skills development

Many of the most active people in the visual thinking field – David Sibbet, Dan Roam, Sunni Brown, Dave Gray, Brandy Agerback, Willemien Brand, Mark Rohde, etc. – and associated businesses like Xplane, Scriberia and so on, increasingly work not just to visually support businesses but also to train and encourage business people to draw for themselves. There is clearly a growing appetite for this, judging from the success of books like Dan Roam's *Back of the Napkin*, Sunni Brown's *Doodle Revolution* and the burgeoning market in visual thinking workshops.

As we saw earlier with SSM-style rich pictures, one of the main barriers people face in creating visuals themselves is the assumption that they can't draw. The approaches taken by most teachers to overcome this are variations on the 'visual alphabet', whereby more complex images are drawn from simpler visual elements (as shown in the example in Figure 4.4), i.e. if people can draw lines then they can draw boxes, if they can draw boxes, they can draw computer screens, etc.

In our experience, the most significant factor for getting people drawing is the extent to which they appreciate the value of meaning over aesthetics. Showing workshop participants that a series of stick people joined together by arrows and bubbles is still likely to convey more meaning about system behaviour than a block of text – even if the quality of finish

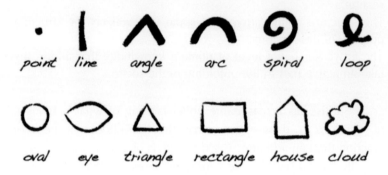

Figure 4.4 Examples from a visual alphabet
Reproduced with permission from O'Reilly Media, Inc.[15]

does resemble something from a kindergarten – encourages them to have a go themselves, without worrying about being judged.

Visual process support techniques

Many of the key people associated with visual thinking have gone on to develop structured workshopping techniques with standardised visual components. David Sibbet, for example, and his company The Grove Consultants, have long complemented their visual consultancy practice by selling a range of templates with associated instructions for supporting a range of meeting types and outcomes.

Dave Gray, Sunni Brown and James Macanufo collected a range of over 80 group techniques in their popular book *Gamestorming*,[16] ranging from mainstream business and design exercises such as Force Field Analysis and the Business Model Canvas to more eclectic facilitative techniques invented by the authors. By calling these techniques 'games', the authors present group workshops as a sequence of 'plays', designed and adapted by the facilitators to meet the workshop objectives (see Figure 4.5).

Their book assumes the use of visual language to bind the exercises together, and devotes much of its preliminary material to basic drawing techniques. It has therefore become not just a popular reference book for

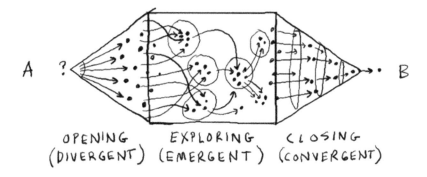

OPENING   EXPLORING   CLOSING
(DIVERGENT)   (EMERGENT)   (CONVERGENT)

Figure 4.5 Gamestorming – example flow
Reproduced with permission from O'Reilly Media, Inc.[17]

consultants wanting to become more visual in their practice, but an inspiration for graphic recorders seeking to upskill and market themselves as event designers and facilitators.

We explore template-based visuals and the visual language associated with them more fully in the next chapter.

The role of the facilitator

Although we have been alluding to this throughout the chapter, it's worth stressing the crucial importance of the facilitator when deploying any of these techniques. This is not just about their ability to maintain the consistency and quality of visual language, but also about the feeling in the room, the quality of the set-up, and most important of all, the quality of questioning.

In order to maximise the shared meaning in the room, the facilitator needs to find the appropriate balance between the different 'dialects' of the communities represented. We tend to assume that when someone else uses a familiar word it must mean the same to them as it does to us, even though in practice this is never completely true. So it's crucial that the facilitator keeps checking what the *shared experience* is that the words are pointing to. In all of the live picture-making approaches we have seen in this chapter (and the live templated and diagramming approaches we will see in the next two chapters), the visuals are a proxy that helps to achieve this aim. If simple words like 'service', 'system' or 'customer satisfaction' can mean such different things to different communities, then having a picture or icon next to them when they are recorded can disambiguate the meaning. But this meaning isn't produced in a vacuum! If a graphic recorder simply records what they think is meant using generic or non-committal imagery, there is no shared meaning and the graphics will probably be ignored during the flow of the conversation. The onus rests on the *facilitator* to intervene and ask clarifying questions, in order to ensure that it is the *shared* meaning that is recorded.

The key skill here is the ability to 'dis-abstract' the language people use, reconnecting it back to the experiences that it is derived from. What this means in practice is asking for examples, asking what abstract ideas would actually look like when implemented, breaking complex ideas down into more concrete concepts, role-playing, using props and so on. It also means, as we will explore more in the next chapter, starting with templates that can already 'carry' some of the shared meaning before the conversation begins.

Notes

1 Berg, Tessa (2013). *Understanding Iconography: A Method to Allow Rich Picture Interpretation to Improve*. Edinburgh: Heriot Watt University, https://pdfs.semanticscholar.org/b0f3/25a52ad0540f1fd1ece7e43dd2ce627b1645.pdf, accessed July 29, 2019.
2 Rucci, Anthony J., Kirn, Steven P. and Quinn, Richard T. (January–February 1998). The employee-customer-profit chain at Sears. *Harvard Business Review*, https://hbr.org/1998/01/the-employee-customer-profit-chain-at-sears, accessed July 29, 2019.
3 Bell, S., Berg, T. and Morse, S. (2016). *Rich Pictures: Encouraging Resilient Communities*. New York: Routledge.
4 Ibid., pp. 102–103.
5 Engaging for success; enhancing performance through employee engagement. A report to Government by David MacLeod and Nita Clarke, https://dera.ioe.ac.uk/1810/1/file52215.pdf, accessed July 29, 2019.
6 Ibid., p. 9.
7 Ibid.
8 Chris Shipton by Sebastiaan ter Burg, CC BY 4.0, https://creativecommons.org/licenses/by/4.0/.
9 A Graphic Facilitation Retrospective, David Sibbet, http://davidsibbet.com/wp-content/uploads/2016/12/GF-RetrospectiveUpdated.pdf, accessed July 29, 2019, p. 1.

10 Sibbet, David (2010). *Visual Meetings: How Graphics, Sticky Notes & Idea Mapping Can Transform Group Productivity*. Hoboken, NJ: John Wiley & Sons, p. 5.

11 The Grove Consultants International, www.grove.com/, accessed July 29, 2019.

12 Agerback, B. (2012). *The Graphic Facilitator's Guide*. Loosetooth.com Library, p. 9.

13 Bird, K. (2018). *Generative Scribing: A Social Art of the 21st Century*. Cambridge, MA: PI Press, p. 2.

14 Agerback, B. (2016). *The Idea Shapers*. Loosetooth.com Library, p. 2.

15 Figure adapted from *Gamestorming: A Playbook for Innovators, Rulebreakers, and Changemakers*. Sebastopol, CA: O'Reilly Media, Inc. Copyright © 2010 Dave Gray, Sunni Brown and James Macanufo. All rights reserved. Used with permission.

16 Gray, D., Brown, S. and Macanufo, J. (2010). *Gamestorming: A Playbook for Innovators, Rulebreakers, and Changemakers*. Sebastopol, CA: O'Reilly Media, Inc.

17 Figure adapted from *Gamestorming: A Playbook for Innovators, Rulebreakers, and Changemakers*. Sebastopol, CA: O'Reilly Media, Inc. Copyright © 2010 Dave Gray, Sunni Brown and James Macanufo. All rights reserved. Used with permission.

5 Templates and ad hoc visuals

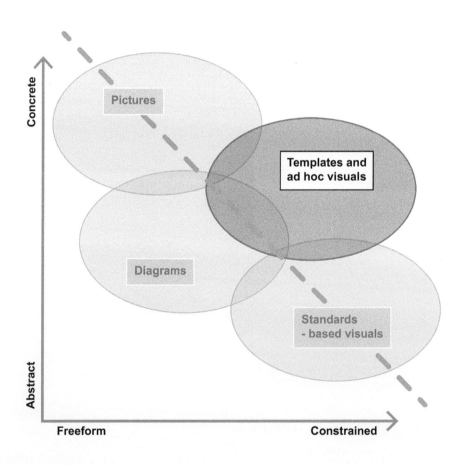

As we approach the mid-point of the Continuum, it's interesting to notice how the models at either end tend to be more 'professionalised': the project or change manager needs to hire professional artists to scribe or create rich pictures, and technical specialists to build architectural models, process maps and technical system designs. Halfway along the Continuum though, the vast majority of the models that are actually created and used are non-professional, non-standards-based, idiosyncratic visual diagrams built either on a one-off basis to an individual style, or following a templated structure given in advance. The notation used is defined by the creator, although boxes and lines are the common choice, with over-lays added as required.

In this chapter we will look at ad hoc visuals and those created using existing templates or frameworks (where there is freedom of language, but using a pre-determined overall composition), and in the next chapter we will look at more structured diagramming approaches (where there is freedom of overall composition, but using a pre-determined visual lan-guage). We will also explore the idea of 'visual fitness', i.e. why some diagrams seem to spread across organisations while others don't.

Mainstream frameworks and visual fitness

Some frameworks are so ubiquitous that they have become a standard part of the management lexicon. Take the SWOT analysis as an example. SWOT analyses are usually performed in business change to weigh up the pros and cons of the current state and/or competing options for the future.

We have occasionally seen the acronym reversed ('TOWS' instead of 'SWOT'), but what is almost never changed is the *appearance* of the model – the four categories presented in a 2 × 2 matrix shown in Figure 5.1.

If someone says 'let's do a SWOT analysis', it usually means drawing two crossed lines on a flipchart or whiteboard, and filling in the boxes. There are three interesting things to say about this.

Firstly, the visual language of the boxes carries no significant addi-tional meaning. The lines 'disguise' the fact that underneath the boxes are just lists of words. In some ways they confuse it, because they seem to imply a clear separation between all four concepts, like a cake sliced into four separate pieces, whereas in reality the four concepts are not

Figure 5.1 SWOT analysis template

clear and distinct in this way. Most people read the Strengths and Weaknesses as internal, and the Opportunities and Threats as external, but there is nothing in the visual language to indicate this. For example, should a high level of customer brand recognition be classified as a *strength* of the company or an *opportunity* for market exploitation? Maybe it's actually a *threat*, because it's been known in the past to lead to complacency, which is a *weakness*. More generally, how many corporate failures have arisen from leadership teams failing to recognise that market forces have converted their greatest strengths into their greatest weaknesses?

Secondly, although it's hard to quantify, surely a huge proportion of the value of a familiar framework like SWOT is not in the contents or structure at all, but in the very fact of its familiarity. When facing uncertainty as a group, familiar frameworks help to resolve anxiety and create a sense of shared direction. There is an element of social proofing here, i.e. 'if a SWOT analysis is what everyone does in planning situations then it must be the right thing to do'.

These two points together suggest a third, more interesting conclusion, which is that the visual language of a ubiquitous framework like a SWOT grid may do little to improve its inherent meaning or usefulness, but persist nevertheless because it makes the framework more memorable, familiar and/or easy to reproduce. Richard Dawkins[1] invented the term 'meme' to describe ideas as analogous to genes, impacted by forces of selection in the same way that biological organisms are. If we see management models as memes, a memorable visual representation adds to the differential 'fitness' of one model over another.

Numerous examples of this 'visual fitness' come to mind: would Ishikawa diagrams (shown in Figure 5.2 and discussed in the next chapter) have become so popular had someone not noticed their resemblance to fish skeletons? The resemblance to a fish is entirely coincidental and carries no additional meaning, but renaming the technique 'fishbone analysis' hugely improves the diagram's survival chances, because it is so much more memorable than 'Ishikawa'.

The wavy lines of the Cynefin sense-making framework (see Figure 5.3) developed by Dave Snowden and Cynthia Kurtz[2] aim to communicate that the content in each domain is dynamic, not fixed, but in so doing they also visually stand apart from the fixed lines and boxes of most other frameworks, improving the diagram's visual fitness in the ecology of management frameworks.

Michael Porter could have simply listed his famous Five Forces when he first presented them in 1979, but their subsequent evolution

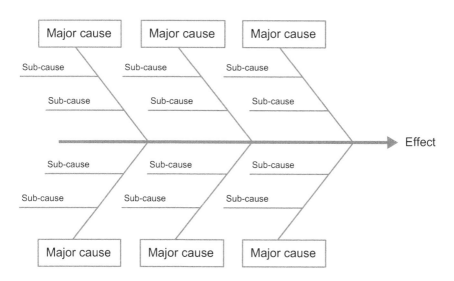

Figure 5.2 An Ishikawa diagram template

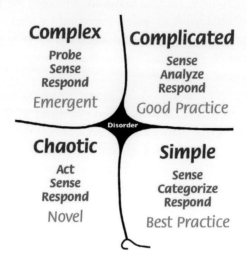

Figure 5.3 The Cynefin sense-making framework
Reproduced under licence.[3]

into one of the most widely used strategic frameworks of the past 40 years is hard to imagine without the diagram that accompanied them, which is normally drawn in strategy workshops as a template similar to the one shown in Figure 5.4. Porter later revealed that his model was a direct response to SWOT:

> The prevailing SWOT model … was based on the idea that every case is different and that the relevant considerations are company-specific. As I was struggling to teach using the SWOT framework at HBS, I set out to add more rigor.[4]

Unlike the SWOT framework, the visual 'fitness' of the diagram arises not just from its simplicity of content and form, but from the resonance between the visual language and the underlying conceptual structure.

Once again, the model's survival as an enduring strategy exercise is at least partly down to how simply it can be drawn, but look at the visual logic of the box locations in contrast to the arbitrariness of the SWOT framework. It is intuitive for participants modelling their competitive position to put themselves and their competitors in the centre of the diagram. Putting sellers and buyers along a row from left to right models the chronology of the

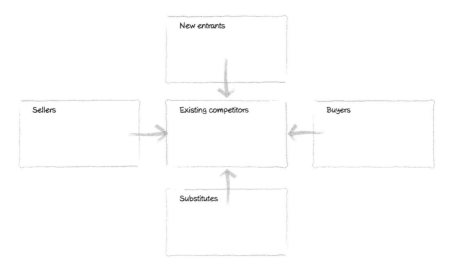

Figure 5.4 A template of Porter's Five Forces model

industry's supply chain, as the model's (at the time) predominantly Western readers read time from left to right. Potential new entrants and potential substitutes are then arranged orthogonally to this flow, which makes sense, as the forces they exert are through their potential rather than actual interaction with the industry. Whether this composition is by accident or design, there is no doubt in our minds that the 'resonance' thus created between the visual language of the diagram and the conceptual structure of the model goes some way to explaining why it became so popular.

We look at this idea of visual resonance in more detail in the next section, but it is useful to have this example as a touch point in order to contrast other familiar models. The Porter illustration is an example of the usual pattern of where templates come from: a recognised authority produces a model or framework, which is turned into a visually memorable diagram, which is then used as a basis for capturing content in workshops. The reason for stressing the idea of 'visual fitness' here is to encourage a more critical attitude to the visual language that is used. The visual language of the Five Forces makes the underling logic of that model clearer and more memorable. Now contrast this with another popular management diagram, the McKinsey 7S model, shown in Figure 5.5. As with the Five Forces, when this framework is used in change workshops, content is typically captured as a list of words under each of the categories, in order to model the future state that the participants want to achieve. The framework itself though is universally identified by its visual representation as an arrangement of 'bubbles':

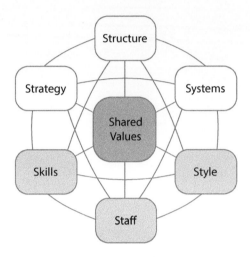

Figure 5.5 Example of the McKinsey 7S model

By our broad definition, this is clearly a model, in that it is a simplified representation of a complex reality. But for most people looking at the actual content, it is really a list of elements arranged in a circle. The only additional meaning provided by the visual language is the centrality of one of the elements and the fact that everything is connected to everything else. This is interesting to represent, but it's also a simple truism – everything *is* connected to everything else. We have never seen anyone use the lines to capture content in a workshop – how systems affect strategy, how structure affects style and so on (which would probably be a lot more interesting – though even just looking at the pairs of concepts would add another 21 concepts!). If you look at the text of the many management books in which this framework is cited, the structure of the list becomes obvious, as the elements are described sequentially:

- Hard elements:

    - Strategy;
    - Structure;
    - Systems.

- Soft elements:

  - Staff;
  - Skills;
  - Style.

- Central element:

  - Shared values.

We conclude that the arrangement of the elements as bubbles in the diagram is adding little to the underlying content. We could go further and – as with the SWOT table – point out that the separation of the terms into bubbles is actually misleading, because so much of the content would naturally belong in multiple bubbles. What if we are talking about the *skills* that *staff* need in order to create a *strategy* for future *systems*? If we were to actually map out real-life 7S content in a way that was visually representative, we would end up with a complex Venn Diagram, not seven neatly separated bubbles. The model has endured not just because it lists things that people want to talk about, but because it comes from an authoritative source (McKinsey), is memorable (the 'S' mnemonic, the 'Seven S' alliteration), and has a visual layout that is immediately identifiable. It has *not* endured because the graphic is adding visual meaning to the bare list of concepts.

At least the basic list from which the diagram is derived does have a degree of structure – a two-level taxonomy that has then been reflected in the colour contrast of the bubbles in the model. Many of the frameworks invented by smaller consultancies or by organisations for internal use have literally no structure; they are simply an unordered list of concepts. Figure 5.6 gives a typical example.

The shapes and colour are doing all the work here – imbuing a sense of substance in what is essentially just a list of words, and in so doing increasing the visual fitness of what is subsequently described as a 'framework'. The colours and shapes create the *impression* of meaning but actually add none. What they do accomplish is to 'brand' the list so that it's instantly recognisable. There is nothing wrong with making a list of concepts memorable if it's an important list for everyone to remember, but if the list itself has little meaning, then the visual memorability sets up a dissonance in the viewer between the apparent significance of what

Figure 5.6 A visual list

their eyes are seeing and the lack of substance in the concepts their minds are absorbing. If (as is often the case) the visually memorable device is created by the corporate graphics department using the company's internal brand guidelines, then surely the company runs a risk of having its visual identity associated in employees' minds with vagueness or meaninglessness.

In case you feel that we are doing an injustice to Figure 5.6, we should point out that we concocted this diagram ourselves and chose the concepts at random! The reason diagrams like this exist is because they typically start out as a series of bullet points on a flipchart during a brainstorming session. Without going further and understanding the inter-relationships between the concepts, there is no meaning to express visually. The graphic designer charged with 'modellising' the concepts is not paid (and often has no desire) to understand the relationships between them, so faithfully transposes them into a colourful diagram without challenging the lack of meaning.

What is the relevance of this to organisational transformation? In our experience, there are usually one or two core diagrams that become central focal points for everyone involved in the programme or initiative. These may be based on well-known templates, such as the ones we have been looking at in this section, they may come from proprietary transformation models supplied by consultancy partners, or they may have been generated internally by the organisation itself. All too often these diagrams take on a life of their own, and are referenced by everyone on the assumption that they *mean* the same thing to everyone, without this assumption ever being tested. And so it is worthwhile to always ask what the true drivers of the ecological 'fitness' of a particular model are: does the underlying model *actually* mean the same thing to everyone, or is a lack of shared meaning being disguised by colourful graphics?

Visual resonance

How does one go about answering the above question? We address this in more detail in Chapter 9, but here we look at some less ambiguous examples of popular models where the underlying meaning of the concepts has been enriched by the visual language of the diagram.

Take Maslow's Hierarchy of Needs, another ubiquitous model that is frequently referenced in culture change projects. We're not interested here in the merits of the actual model, but in the way that it's presented, which is typically something like Figure 5.7.

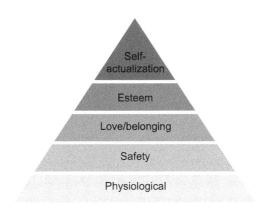

Figure 5.7 Maslow's Hierarchy of Needs

We previously criticised models for being 'lists in disguise'. But this is clearly not just a list: the verticality of the diagram represents levels of dependency in a hierarchy – the upper blocks would not be there without the lower ones to rest on. If you switched the order here, it would *mean* something different. The closest you can get in text is an ordered list:

1   Physiological needs;
2   Safety needs;
3   Love and belonging needs;
4   Esteem needs;
5   Self-actualisation needs.

But of course, the point of the model is not that the elements are discrete, but that they form a chain of dependency – Maslow was arguing that you can't meet one level of need without satisfying all the needs below it. Saying that they're ordinal and putting them into a chronological list, as above, ends up visually inverting the order of the pyramid. The difficulty of explaining this in words is actually making the point for us: the visual language of the pyramid is conveying meaning to the viewer on an instinctive level that would take a paragraph to fully explain verbally. It *resonates* with the conceptual structure, because both the hierarchy and the pyramid share gravity as an underlying metaphor: everyone experiences gravity as a downward force, and support as therefore coming from underneath, so showing the list as a pyramid of elements gives us the 'dependency' meaning for free, as shown in Figure 5.8.

Meanings like these are implicit in the visual language of diagrams whether their creators are aware of them or not. Imagine, for instance, if the pyramid was turned upside down. We have actually seen a number of instances of this happening, where progressive leadership teams have tried to instigate cultural change in their organisations by inverting their org charts, in order to position the leadership role as *supporting* the organisation, not the other way around. Because org charts are generally shaped as pyramids, this reversal results in an upside-down triangle, as shown in Figure 5.9.

The support metaphor still works here, because of the implicit force of gravity working downwards. These diagrams seem unlikely though, not just because gravity makes it appear that the organisation will fall over, but because another basic meaning of verticality is that power comes from

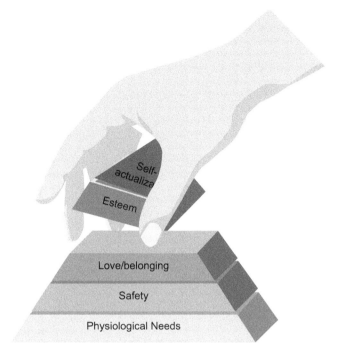

Figure 5.8 A pyramid as a visual structure

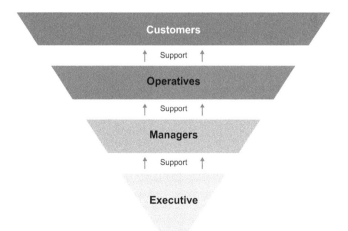

Figure 5.9 An inverted pyramid

above (because in the world, stronger things are typically larger than us). It is hard to imagine that, as a result of seeing this kind of diagram, employees would immediately reverse the meanings of, say, 'overseeing' and 'working under'; the 'up is power' metaphor is simply too strongly engrained.

It's interesting to notice in passing that Maslow's pyramid was not actually created by Maslow. His Hierarchy of Needs was just a list in his original 1943 paper; the pyramid appears to have been created by a consultant – Charles McDermid for his 1960 article 'How Money Motivates Men' in *Business Horizons*.[5] This is not uncommon; the subsequent visuals can seem almost as powerful as the academic papers that preceded them.

So visual language can convey meaning that is very hard to illustrate using text alone, even when this meaning is not always what the creators intended. Another simple example is the 2×2 matrix beloved of consultants around the world, which adds a huge amount of meaning over the corresponding words. Here we are referring to 2×2 matrices where the vertical and horizontal have specific meanings, not examples like the SWOT analysis given earlier in the chapter, where a vertical and a horizontal line are simply being used as a convenient device to list concepts under four headings.

The information contained in a Boston Grid, for example (Figure 5.10), where workshop participants chart their products and services against growth and share, would be incredibly hard to represent using words alone.

Probably the most influential piece of visual language in business change in recent years has been Alexander Osterwalder's Business Model Canvas (Figure 5.11),[6] which has been used by organisations to understand their current range of business models, and the business models they want to develop in the future. It has also spawned a whole genre of 'canvas' products – templates produced by niche consultancies to assist clients with whatever objectives they are pursuing relevant to that niche.

The Business Model Canvas is, in essence, a classification framework which is agnostic to industry or type of business, comprising nine constituents defined as Building Blocks (Key Partnerships, Key Activities, etc.). It is defined as being 'a shared language for describing, visualising, assessing, and changing business models'.[7]

Figure 5.10 The Boston Grid

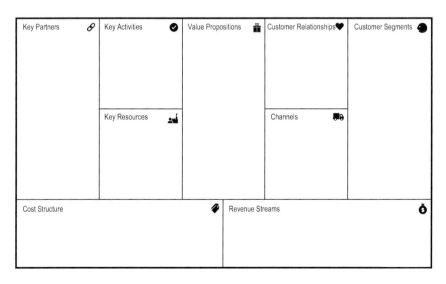

Figure 5.11 The Business Model Canvas

Reproduced with permission from John Wiley & Sons.

Visually, the Business Model Canvas has at its centre the value proposition. This balances the supply elements (partners, activities, resources) and costs with the demand elements (channels, customer relationships, customer segments) and revenues.

What is most interesting here, given what we have already said in this chapter, is just how much meaning is lost if the visualisation is reduced to just a list of words:

- Key activities;
- Value proposition;
- Customer relationships;
- And so on …

We discuss the Canvas further in Chapter 9 and include (in Figures 9.2 and 9.3) more visual forms of it.

The Business Model Canvas is a perfect example of the kind of visual resonance that can exist between the underlying concepts of a model and the visual language used in the diagram or template that illustrates it. It is this resonance that determines the ability of some diagrams to engender a shared feeling of 'I get that' in an audience, the sense of shared meaning that we have been emphasising as the cornerstone of organisational agility. We will explore this sense of resonance and how it can be created in more detail in Chapter 9.

Common models

Operating models

The popularity of Osterwalder's work has brought the word 'canvas' into mainstream business parlance as a more design-inspired word for 'template', and spawned a raft of other canvases, produced by individuals and small consultancies eager to replicate Osterwalder's success. One interesting recent example of this is the Operating Model Canvas (Figure 5.12) produced by Andrew Campbell and colleagues of Ashridge Business School in the UK. Notice how it explicitly 'plugs into' Osterwalder's canvas, as can be seen from the introduction to his book on the subject.[8] It makes sense for readers of Campbell's book to start with something

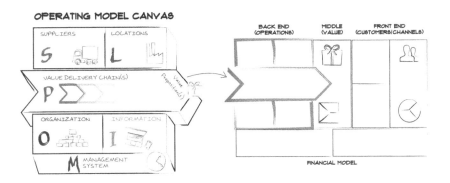

Figure 5.12 Operating Model Canvas

Reproduced with permission from Andrew Campbell and Van Haren Publishing.

familiar in order to give context for what follows. These are the conse-quences of a particular model becoming a mainstream standard: it creates an extremely valuable pool of shared meaning. If we return to Dawkins' reframing of ideas as memes, the Business Model Canvas is like a dominant species in the ecosystem of business frameworks – other models gain fitness by coupling with it.

Campbell is trying to create a standard format for what is one of the most common non-standard visualisations in organisational change. There will be very few major transformation programmes that do not have an operating model workstream trying to produce an operating model dia-gram. An operating model is simply a high-level description of how an organisation works or needs to work. Change is traditionally broken down into something along the lines of 'people', 'processes' and 'technology', so the operating model exists to show how all these components combine to create value. Typically, there will be an 'as is' model, a 'to be' model and a gap analysis of what needs to change to get from one to the other. The 'to be' model is often called the 'target' operating model, hence the acronym 'TOM'. In practice, these diagrams almost invariably boil down to one or two presentation slides containing colourful boxes, arrows and words. There is no canonical form for what this diagram should look like, which is the gap that Campbell is seeking to fill with his model.

One of the best (certainly one of the most theoretically rigorous) approaches to designing (or diagnosing problems in) an operating model is to use the Viable System Model (VSM)[9] of Stafford Beer[10] (Figure 5.13), which we mentioned in Chapter 3. Although it is over 50 years old, it still has a sizeable following, particularly among systems-oriented consultants and practitioners. Whether or not you agree with our evaluation, the reason we include the model in this chapter is to point out that regardless of the inherent merits of VSM as an approach, it is Beer's own diagram that has probably done more than anything else to stop the model entering the mainstream, due to its overwhelming visual complexity. This is very much at odds with the relative simplicity of the underlying model, as shown in simplified form in Figure 3.8.

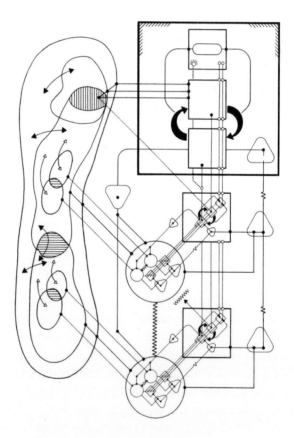

Figure 5.13 Beer's final depiction of the VSM

Reproduced with permission from John Wiley & Sons.

Beer actually devoted an entire appendix of one of his books to explaining why the diagram should not be altered, yet it is the detail and exactitude of his visual language that has, perhaps, precluded it becoming a focal point for shared meaning in the way other models in this chapter have. In a memetic sense it may have 'theoretical' fitness, but it is very much lacking in 'visual' fitness.

Processes and journeys

The examples so far in this chapter have all been of high-level strategic and operational content. By volume though, the majority of templated and ad hoc diagrams produced to support transformation are to do with flows – tracing organisational processes, interactions, customer journeys and so on.

SIPOC diagrams – used in lean manufacturing, Six Sigma and other process improvement methods – are a way of showing all the constituents of an end-to-end process. The diagrams model the **S**uppliers to the

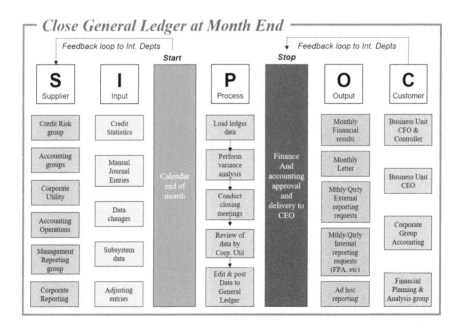

Figure 5.14 A SIPOC diagram
Reproduced with permission from ASQ.[11]

process, the process **I**nputs, the **P**rocess itself, the process **O**utputs and the **C**ustomers of the outputs. SIPOC is a recognised structure, but there is no standardised way of visualising it. Figure 5.14 shows an example template diagram.

Linked with internal roles and business functions, the architecture can demonstrate who performs what process. Business processes can also be linked with technology, e.g. business applications, to connect the business architecture with more specialist technology architectures.

Interaction modes are another example; they represent the interactions and dependencies between elements, usually structural elements, modelling the collaboration between organisations (B2B), between organisations and customers (B2C) and, in software engineering, between software components. They may also be modelled showing a specific context such as the services being deployed to realise the interaction or the information flow between the elements, or both.

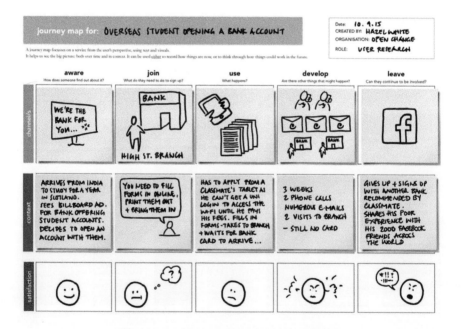

Figure 5.15 An example Customer Journey Map

Reproduced with permission from Open Change.[12]

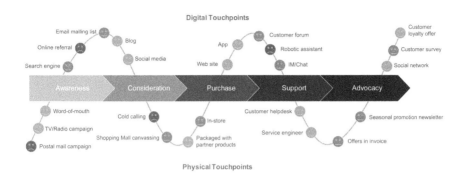

Figure 5.16 A Customer Journey Map with touchpoints

Customer Journey Models (or Customer Journey Maps, Customer Experience Maps, Customer Experience Models, etc.) are a staple, particularly of design-led approaches to change (see Chapter 3). A key feature of customer journey models is that they show the alignment (or misalignment) of organisations with the services offered to customers, helping to overcome the functional silos that tend to inhibit seamless customer experience of those services. They are also valuable when re-engineering businesses and when designing new products and services. A current-state Customer Journey Model may show the adverse experience of customers – see, for example, Figure 5.15.

The customer's journey is visualised from left to right (with the underlying structure being the customer lifecycle itself). The visual relies heavily on the use of text to describe the context. A variant of Figure 5.15 is Figure 5.16 which shows the 'touchpoints' at which there is an interaction between the customer and the organisation overlaid onto a customer lifecycle, and a happy/indifferent/sad face shows the organisation's assessment of the status of each touchpoint.

Notes

1 Dawkins, R. (2006). *The Selfish Gene*. Oxford: Oxford University Press.
2 Kurtz, Cynthia F. and Snowden, David J. (2003). The new dynamics of strategy: Sense-making in a complex and complicated world. *IBM Systems Journal*, 42(3), pp. 462–83.
3 Cynefin framework by Dave Snowden, CC BY3.0, https://creativecommons.org/licenses/by/3.0.

4 Porter, Michael, Argyres, Nicholas and McGahan, Anita M. (2002). An interview with Michael Porter. *The Academy of Management Executive*, 16(2), (May), p. 43.

5 Bridgman, T., Cummings, S. and Ballard, J. (2019). Who built Maslow's pyramid? A history of the creation of management studies' most famous symbol and its implications for management education. *Academy of Management Learning & Education*, 18(1), pp. 81–98.

6 Osterwalder, A. and Pigneur, Y. (2010). *Business Model Generation*. Hoboken, NJ: John Wiley & Sons.

7 Ibid., p. 12.

8 Campbell, A., Gutierrez, M. and Lancelott, M. (2017). *Operating Model Canvas*. Zaltbommel: Van Haren Publishing.

9 The Viable System Model (VSM) is a model of the organisational structure of any autonomous system capable of producing itself. A viable system is any system organised in such a way as to meet the demands of surviving in the changing environment.

10 Beer, S. (1985). *Diagnosing the System for Organizations*. Chichester: John Wiley.

11 American Society for Quality. © 2019 ASQ, www.asq.org. All rights reserved. No further distribution allowed without permission.

12 www.openchange.co.uk, accessed July 29, 2019.

Diagrams

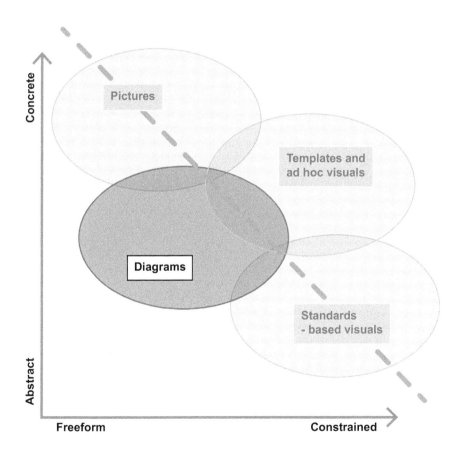

We would need several books to list, describe and give examples of all the named diagramming techniques that exist in the world, and they would immediately be out of date upon publication! Instead, we want to survey a representative sample that illustrates the progression from the kind of free-flow visualisation we saw in rich pictures through to more structured techniques, stopping just short of the internationally standardised models we explore in the next chapter.

In the following sections we discuss the diagrams in order of ascending level of structure. These are loosely defined categories we have created for convenience; what we are really describing is a continuum.

Unstructured diagramming

We start with diagrams that have no formalised conventions at all, which probably represent the majority of diagrams scribbled on office white-boards during impromptu brainstorming sessions, such as in Figure 6.1.

This 'intuitive' level of diagramming involves all the same basic elements (words, shapes, arrows, lines) as the formalised techniques we are

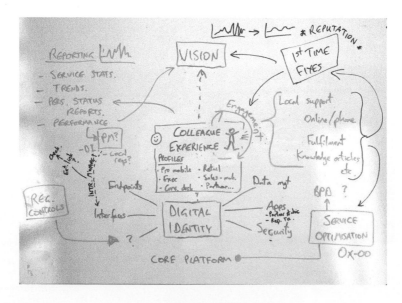

Figure 6.1 A typical whiteboard diagram

about to describe, so it's useful to remember how much meaning comes 'for free', even without the conventions; people do not need to be told that a word with a shape around it represents a concept, or that lines represent relationships between those concepts. What is at stake is how well the model creates shared meaning for however many different people from different backgrounds need to use it. If a scribble on a flipchart is only for the use of a single team in a single meeting it doesn't matter so much, but what happens when it needs to be formalised and shared more widely? And even in the room, how do you know that everyone is reading each concept and relationship in the same way?

Often whiteboard diagrams take on a life of their own, once they have been transferred into presentation slides or other diagramming software. It's not uncommon to see detailed system maps like Figure 6.2 being produced during IT-driven transformation. Meaning is bolstered, in part at least, by the inclusion of a key, but even so, some insider knowledge is necessary to fully understand what's going on.

This is what happens when no diagramming conventions are followed: the structure and visual language develop organically and idiosyncrati-cally; each icon has to be explained separately to each new viewer, and although the use of colour adds meaning, it also adds to the overall complexity of the diagram.

Not that conventions are always the answer. Having a pre-agreed visual language builds shared meaning, but at the expense of everyone having to learn that language and use it consistently. This is the main consideration as we progress through each additional level of conventional structure: how much additional shared meaning is created as a result, and does it merit the cost in terms of the restrictions imposed and the need for every-one to learn it? We will provide some reflections and principles for answering these questions at the end of the chapter.

Conventional diagrams

Concept maps and system concept diagrams

Concept maps (see Figure 6.3) were developed by Joseph Novak, an educa-tionalist at Cornell, during the 1970s. Concepts are represented in boxes/bubbles, and relationships by the labelled, arrowed lines between them. The

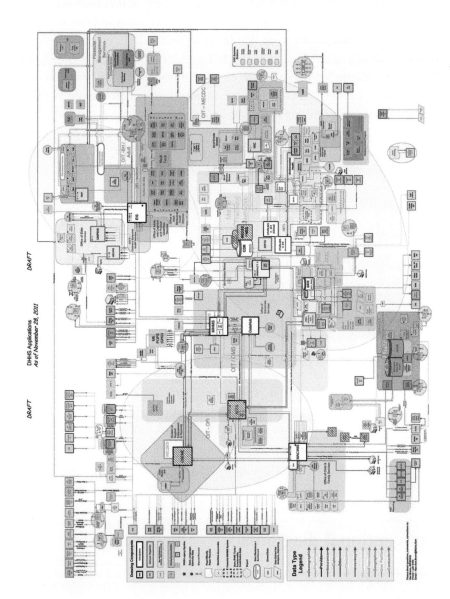

Figure 6.2 A complex, non-standard IT system domain diagram (for illustrative purposes only)[1]

Figure 6.3 A concept map

idea is that any two boxes and lines can be read as a meaningful sentence in the direction of the arrow.

Concept maps are often used by students in learning environments, and are popular as workshop tools for systemic discovery in the early stages of transformation. The definition phase of organisational change is, after all, a learning environment for management. Concept mapping is a quick and easy way to lay out what is known about the situation, and diagramming software makes it very easy to use the technique in live group sessions.

Alongside concept maps are system context diagrams (SCDs). They have their roots in engineering and, like concept maps, summarise a situation, in this case a system and the elements that interact with it. Context diagrams regularly appear when producing data flow diagrams, showing key elements of the system being modelled and data flows to/from it, as shown in the example in Figure 6.4. When people draw diagrams at multiple levels, where each level provides more granular detail of the level above it (its parent diagram), the highest level (sometimes termed Level 0) is usually a context diagram, which defines the boundaries for the system.

Many context diagrams are embellished with colour and other visual aspects to distinguish or emphasise specific elements.

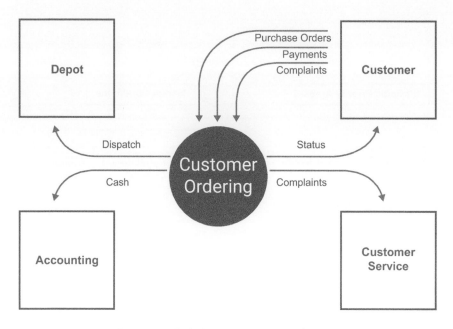

Figure 6.4 Ordering system context diagram

Mind maps

The term 'mind map' (see the example in Figure 6.5) was popularised by Tony Buzanin the 1970s, and although he trademarked the term, the idea of illustrating sub-concepts radially around a central node has been common throughout history. Buzan gives lots of guidelines for how to create mind maps (start with an image, use at least three colours, decrease line weight further from the centre, etc.), which makes it easy to recognise when a map has been created by someone who's read his books. In practice though, most people use the term to refer to any concept map with a single central node, not just a diagram that follows Buzan's instructions.

Spray diagrams

'Spray diagram' is a term sometimes used for a looser, more free-flowing hierarchical map in which the relationships between concepts are not specified, as shown in Figure 6.6.

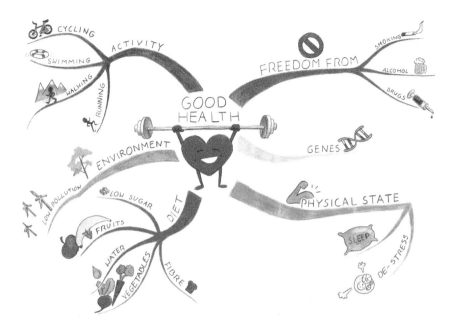

Figure 6.5 A mind map

Although the spray diagram has the same structural form as a mind map (a radially arranged conceptual hierarchy), the distinction seems to be that while the hierarchy in the mind map tends to represent a necessarily hierarchical relation (X is part of Y, X is an example of Y, etc.), a spray diagram is simply a loose chain of associations. In practice, this is probably what most brainstorming sessions look like when the facilitator starts to produce a mind map.

We begin with these three diagram types (concept maps, mind maps and spray diagrams) because they have canonical definitions associated with them (Buzan 1974;[2] Novak[3] 1998), yet if we were to forget the labels and look at how they are actually used in practice, what are the differences? For example:

- When creating mind maps, people often use lines and arrows and boundary markers to depict non-hierarchical relationships. Most mind mapping software allows relationships to be drawn across nodes in this way. Are the resulting diagrams still mind maps, even if they look more like concept maps?

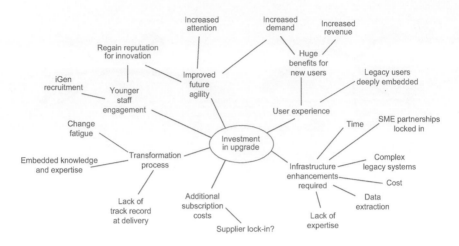

Figure 6.6 Spray diagram

- Concept maps are often drawn with labels missing from arrows, so they look more like spray diagrams. Which are they?
- A meeting facilitator writes a central topic on a whiteboard and starts recording contributions around it. They call it a mind map, even though by the above definition it is a spray diagram, a term they've never heard of. Who is right – the facilitator or Tony Buzan?

Add to this the fact that different communities and individuals clearly use different names to refer to the same kinds of diagrams, just as we have already seen with rich pictures. What is the difference between a concept map and a concept diagram? Or a relationship map? Or a relationship diagram? Or a conceptual relationship map? If a concept map is created with pictures accompanying each of the words, does that make it a rich picture?

A big part of the problem is that names are rarely neutral – there are often commercial and intellectual interests at stake. Buzan's protection of the term 'mind map' is a case in point. In 2013, Boardman and Sauser[4] published a book in which they described the concept of a 'systemigram', a visual map produced in SystemiTool, a downloadable software program developed by the authors. An example of a systemigram is shown in Figure 6.7.

How is this different to Novak's concept maps, beyond a greater freedom to nest concepts inside shapes to show containment relationships? If

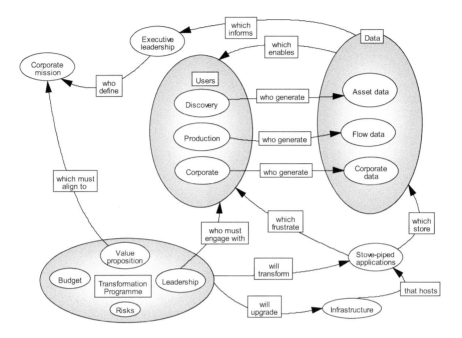

Figure 6.7 A systemigram

someone drawing a concept map on a flipchart nests one or more concepts, does it become a systemigram? Or if a systemigram lacks nesting, does it become a concept map? Who gets to decide what the canonical names should be, when there are no international standards for free-flow modelling as there are for more structured modelling languages like UML and BPMN?

This might seem absurd, but it serves to highlight the fluidity that exists between free-flow diagramming techniques, and how many of the names and definitions are based not on practice or provenance but other, more human concerns.

Systems diagrams

What all these techniques that we have discussed so far in this chapter have in common is that they are modelling relationships between concepts using words and lines, but with very little constraint as to what those relationships and concepts are, or how the words and lines should be formed. However, all the freeform diagrams we look at are based on the same foundations. They are simply adding more constraints.

For example, we can add the constraint that all the arrows represent influences, in order to create an influence diagram – see Figure 6.8. In small group workshops and informal settings, this is as far as the visual language usually needs to go.

Influence diagrams like these are usually used to help a group build up a model of the system at a point in time. Many facilitators who use these kinds of informal influence maps will add meaning through additional elements of visual language – using thicker lines for stronger influences, codifying influence types through different line colours and creating containing shapes to show system boundaries, for example. However, these are informal conventions.

There is nothing intrinsic to the visual language that says that the arrows have to represent influence, so the onus is on the facilitator to hold the

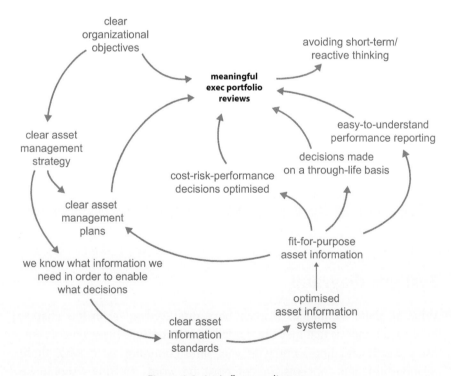

Figure 6.8 An influence diagram

group to task. Participants will often suggest relationships that are more about time than influence – causality, flow of goods and materials, sequence of events, for example – whereas the point of the diagram is to show the current state of the system, not how it is changing over time.

This description of an influence diagram is the one that will be familiar to systems practitioners and educators.[5] It's interesting to contrast this with how the same term is used by decision analysts, for whom an 'Influence Diagram' is a type of formal path diagram, originally developed by Howard and Matheson[6] at Stanford in the 1980s, but still popular today. Here the visual language is much more constrained; decisions are rectangles, variables are rounded rectangles, objectives are hexagons, uncertainties are ovals and circular references are not allowed; Figure 6.9 provides an example.

To a typical trained systems practitioner or group facilitator, this visual language probably seems too prescriptive when working with a non-technical group. So it's interesting to contrast this response to that of the eminent computer scientist Judea Pearl,[7] who in 2005 wrote about why Influence Diagrams (IDs) in this more constrained form lost their appeal:

I could not appreciate why the Stanford group was excited about IDs when they did not compute anything interesting with those

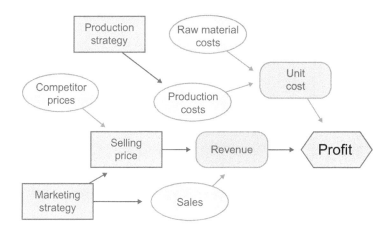

Figure 6.9 A decision Influence Diagram

diagrams, and did not even use the diagram to infer independencies that were not already assumed in its construction.[8]

This is a good example of the paradigms implicit in the Continuum, where the same term has very different connotations depending on which end of the Continuum one is coming from. The problem is not that one approach is better or worse than the other, but that the two paradigms are often running in parallel, unaware of one another's existence. We return to this at the end of the chapter.

Here's a different constraint: instead of making the arrows represent influences, we could constrain them to represent causes, which takes us into another species of diagram, variously called causal maps, causal diagrams, multiple cause diagrams, causal loop diagrams and so on.

To start with, let's look at the causal map format proposed by Ackerman and Eden[9] in their Strategic Options Development and Analysis (SODA) methodology, which they describe as an approach that 'aims to help groups arrive at a negotiated agreement about how to act to resolve a (problematic) situation'. An example is shown in Figure 6.10.

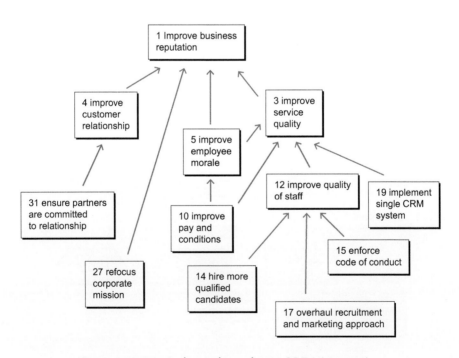

Figure 6.10 A typical causal map from a SODA intervention

Arrows mean 'may lead to', boxes are goals, which are typically at the top ('improve business reputation') and assertions at the bottom. In SODA, these maps are constructed in group exercises, either freehand or using software such as that developed originally by Ackerman and Eden.[10] Bryson et al.[11] give the following reasons for constructing these maps, which could probably be applied to any group diagramming technique:

- To structure thinking through capturing chains of argumentation, dilemmas, etc.;
- To present ideas in a graphical, rather than linear, form;
- To carry out 'rough' analyses;
- To share more easily, through capturing more statements and links on one single A4 page;
- To allow a more 'objective' stance to be taken;
- To capture wisdom, 'tacit' knowledge and experience;
- To improve interviewing capability.

Notice that in order to realise these benefits, once again the onus is on the facilitator to ensure that the meaning of the visual language is understood and observed consistently. The content is all coming from the group, but someone has to ensure that, for example, arrows consistently mean 'X may lead to Y', and not something else like 'X precedes Y' or 'X consists of Y'.

When discussing an open-ended subject, a freeform causal map can become incredibly messy because the content is emerging organically from the group. Someone may observe a series of crucial causal chains between elements that had previously looked unconnected and have been drawn on opposite sides of the page. Soon the most important links get lost in a spaghetti diagram. Messiness of the output in these kinds of sessions is generally not a problem, as the point is to create shared meaning, not a beautiful output! But if the session carries on for too long it's easy for people to get lost, and unless the output is rendered more intelligible soon after the meeting, it too will be consigned to history along with the shared meaning it captured.

One way around this is to add further constraints – forcing a left–right flow of causality along the chain gives us the familiar 'fishbone' diagram (which we mentioned in Chapter 5), making it easier to see what's going on by representing categories of causes as distinct 'branches', though also making it harder to show interdependencies from one branch to another (see Figure 6.11).

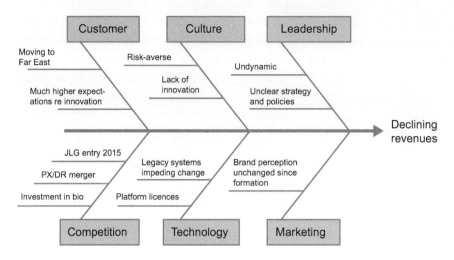

Figure 6.11 A fishbone diagram

A more common solution nowadays is to use diagramming software (often set to 'brainstorming mode') in the live workshop environment, as the elements can be moved around more easily for clarity as the group's understanding of the model evolves. The trouble is, this loses some of the practical, hands-on aspect of the experience – the 'rough and ready' nature of the analysis that Ackerman and Eden allude to. It also limits the group's view of their creation to the size and resolution of the screen.

This tension becomes more obvious as we add more constraints to our diagram examples. The next example (Figure 6.12) is a causal loop diagram, of the type produced by the systems dynamics school of systems thinking, which grew out of the work of Jay Forrester at MIT in the 1960s and 1970s.

In these diagrams, arrows again refer to causality, but this time they are marked as either having a positive or negative effect, shown by the '+' and '–' on the arrowheads. The text is also more constrained, as it must always represent a *variable*, that is, something that can (conceivably) be measured as going up or down. Some modellers prefer to use 'S' and 'O' (for 'same' and 'opposite' direction), instead of '+' and '–', as what's actually being modelled is not an increase or decrease, but whether a change in one variable causes a change in the same direction or in the opposite direction in the affected variable.

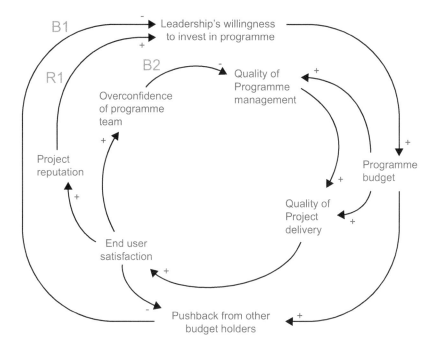

Figure 6.12 A causal loop diagram

The point of these diagrams is to uncover where repeated patterns of individual causal connections in the form of individual feedback loops are yielding higher level patterns of (often unintentional) behaviour in the system. Where the direction of the causal chains in a loop is balanced – i.e. there are the same number of + and – arrows (or O and S) – the loop is labelled 'R' for 'reinforcing'. Its behaviour is self-reinforcing and will – without external interference – grow exponentially, like money in a savings account. If the number of + and – arrows is the same, the loop is labelled 'B' for 'balanced'.

Compared to linear causal diagrams such as the causal maps used in SODA, causal loop diagrams are harder to create in a workshop environment, not so much because they're harder to draw but because they require a greater degree of understanding of the underlying principles and visual language among the participants. When used effectively though, they can be very powerful.

The popularity of causal loop diagrams arose largely from the work of Forrester's student Peter Senge who, in his 1992 book[12] *The Fifth Discipline*, used much-simplified versions of these systems dynamics models to illustrate what he meant by systems thinking. In Senge's diagrams there are no markers on the arrows, and the 'R' and 'B' are replaced with icons of a snowball and a seesaw, like those shown in Figures 6.13 and 6.14 respectively.

Rather than focus on getting people to build complex models of their own, Senge visualised a series of systems 'archetypes', which he and his colleagues turned into templates in a follow-up book, *The Fifth Discipline Fieldbook*.[13] The idea is – as a manager or a team – to become sufficiently familiar with the patterns to be able to guess what is happening from 'inside', i.e. when you are only seeing part of the system.

As we said earlier, all of these free-flow diagramming techniques are really just mechanisms for taking a broader perspective of a complex reality. All of the dynamics that Senge and his colleagues allude to are happening around us every day, but we typically only see a small part of them. By taking a broader perspective, we start to see the broader causes for complex emergent behaviour. We stop repeating the same simple reasons for blaming individuals and start asking where the 'leverage points' are in the overall system.

The other main diagram type associated with systems dynamics is the 'stock and flow' (Figure 6.15), in which certain elements in the causal loop model become 'stocks' (i.e. quantitative variables), and the relationships

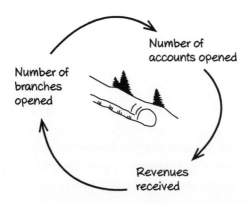

Figure 6.13 A reinforcing loop as a snowball

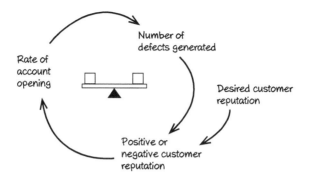

Figure 6.14 A balancing loop as a level seesaw

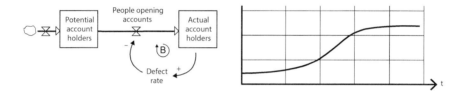

Figure 6.15 Extract of a stock and flow model with time graph

between them are modelled not as simple '+' and '−' but as mathematical functions. These computer-based models can then be used to simulate the behaviour of the system under different base conditions.

We are clearly now well beyond the realms of the generalist facilitator and into the world of the professional modeller, although the fact that the model is represented in a simple graphical form means that models like these are commonly used in workshop environments. A typical process (which might run over a series of weeks) would be to elicit content from the group using dialogue and storytelling techniques, break it down into the core components of the system, use these components with the group to build a causal relationship map, evolve this into a stock and flow diagram with some sensible assumptions about the mathematical relationships, verify with the group that the dynamics of the model seem plausible, then run the simulation under various conditions to determine how best to intervene.

These System Dynamics diagrams occupy an interesting place in our story, bridging the gap from systems diagramming for non-technical group facilitation through to structured mathematical modelling requiring specialist software. As a result, they receive criticism from both sides. Those who see systemic change in a more emergent paradigm criticise it as reductionistic. Jackson[14] summarises this kind of criticism:

> System dynamics misses the point when it tries to study social systems 'objectively', from the outside. And in trying to grasp the complexity of social reality using models built on feedback processes, system dynamics presents itself with an impossible task.

On the other hand, those who see it more in the deterministic paradigm criticise the models for their inaccuracy, and point to more robust mathematical approaches such as Analytic Hierarchy Processes, Markov Chains, Bayesian Belief Networks and so on.

Systems Dynamics adherents will suggest that being attacked from both sides is a sign that they are doing something right – genuinely building a bridge between two extremes. Non-mathematically inclined employees can read a causal loop diagram, but will struggle with a Markov chain. The resulting model may not capture the full complexity of the social system, but then neither can any model! The value is not just about accuracy, but about the conversation that is enabled across organisational boundaries. In our experience, system dynamics models have most often been created as a way of incorporating multiple perspectives into 'quick and dirty' simulations that help managers to rapidly understand recurring patterns of behaviour and explore possible options. The outputs from these inquiries can then feed more formal modelling methods to achieve more robust statistical outputs if required.

Diagramming: a review

There are many more freeform diagramming techniques that we don't have space to describe – value stream maps, effect maps, impact maps, relationship maps, smart maps, scripts maps, giga-maps and the list keeps growing – all with their own names and methodologies and adherents. Each has its uses, but we hope that even the brief survey in this chapter has served to demonstrate how many are really just variations on very similar themes.

How can we choose and get the most from these approaches in the context of business transformation? Here are three general considerations to bear in mind:

- Meaning in the room vs meaning outside the room;
- Freedom vs constraint;
- Software vs freehand.

Meaning in the room vs meaning outside the room

For many of these techniques, the value is not so much in the diagram as in the diagram-*ing*. This is a paradigm shift for many people – that the primary outcome of a meeting can be that a group of people have made sense of something, rather than just produced a tangible piece of paper. The piece of paper on the wall becomes as much about catalysing the subsequent dialogue as about capturing information.

But this immediately raises the question 'what happens next?' A group of people may now have a better understanding of the situation, which will hopefully lead them to make better decisions, but how do those decisions get operationalised? How will the meaning spread if it is only captured in a spaghetti diagram on a huge sheet of paper? This often doesn't get thought through. As with rich pictures, it's all too easy to assume that because the output has a lot of meaning in the room, it must have meaning outside it.

So, if you want to create shared meaning across a broader population, it's worth either choosing a simpler form of diagram, re-building the output of the session in a simpler visual form, or rolling out the diagram creation as an engagement session in its own right.

Freedom vs constraint

This raises the more general point about the appropriate level of constraint in the visual language. We have now been through several levels of this, from whiteboard diagrams through to simple stock and flow models, and the trade-off has hopefully become clear: the more constraints a diagramming technique has, the harder it is to misinterpret the meaning of the diagram, but the greater an onus there is on everyone to use the same constraints, i.e. to *speak the same visual language*. When taken to extremes, this negates the whole point of free-flow diagramming, which is to involve a broader cross-section of stakeholders in a more open-ended conversation.

One thing this highlights, as with the visual thinking approaches we discussed in Chapter 4, is the critical role of the facilitator. The facilitator is not just the custodian of the conversation, but also of the visual language. It is up to the facilitator to clearly explain the rules of the game, and to ensure that they are being correctly observed in order to maintain shared meaning in the group.

When deciding what form of diagramming to use, it's therefore important to ensure that the choice of technique matches the scale and complexity of the challenge. We have stuck to generic diagramming techniques in this chapter, but if the problem is well-specified and restricted to a particular domain (process mapping, data modelling, etc.), then clearly that's the first place to look. But the more open-ended the challenge, the more open-ended a form of diagramming you will probably need to start off with. As you get more information about the nature of the problem, you can then add more constrained diagrams that explore the pertinent aspects of the situation.

It may seem obvious that the more diagramming techniques you practise and feel comfortable with – regardless of what you call them – the better. The ability to move fluidly from one diagram type to another, while explaining the transition clearly if you are working with a group, gives you an additional level of flexibility to explore the problem from different angles.

Software vs freehand

On the whole, when people are diagramming on their own, they tend to do it on a computer, whereas diagramming in groups tends to be with a pen and flipchart/whiteboard. Some of this is undoubtedly down to practicalities: most knowledge workers have a computer on their desks, whereas introducing one to a workshop requires preparation. There are several other downsides to using software in group sessions though, for example:

- Typical projector resolution makes it hard to read small text;
- There is a reduced sense of involvement: all participants probably feel they could stand up and use a pen, but only people with experience/ training can operate the software;
- Although it's hard to describe, for many people there is something about the kinaesthetic experience of making marks that carries meaning in itself. David Sibbet describes graphic language as 'gesture with a pen'[15]– these gestures have meaning that cannot be replicated with a mouse and cursor.

However, there is one huge upside to software, which is that it is *flexible*. Ackerman and Eden, whose causal mapping techniques we described earlier, use a variant of causal mapping that they call 'oval mapping', in which nodes are written on oval slips that can be moved around, a forerunner of the Design Thinkers' embrace of Post-it notes. Moving things around is essential because the meaning of the marks made on the page shifts as the meeting unfolds. A group of elements that felt closely related at the start of the meeting may seem unrelated by the end. Even with movable ovals and Post-it notes, once arrows, lines and boundaries are drawn around and between them, their location is effectively fixed, because the lines can't be erased. Experienced facilitators will avoid making too many fixed marks like this until later in the session. If the session is short, most people can track the chopping and changing and scribbling, but spend too long working on a single large hand-drawn model and the resulting spaghetti will at some point become incoherent and distracting rather than enabling. At this point it's often better to spend a break redrawing the diagram more neatly, but this can take time.

Software removes the problem. If the group makes sense of something in a new and different way, elements can simply be moved around. What people are seeing is a much closer representation of the emerging group consensus. When using mind maps, for example, it's common to want to re-categorise an element and therefore move it to a different node. This is impossible on a piece of paper, but can be done by a simple mouse-drag on a computer.

Modern diagramming software is also starting to blur the boundaries between the techniques described above. Where in the past mind maps, concept maps, influence diagrams, UML and so on each required a different specialist program, by using a more generic modern tool these can merge fluidly in a single session. This obviously offers great power but also puts a greater onus on the person operating the software to make sure that the visual language is still being interpreted in a consistent way by everyone.

Notes

1 Novak, J. D. (1998). *Learning, Creating, and Using Knowledge*. Mahwah, NJ: Lawrence Erlbaum Associates, Inc.
2 Buzan, T. (1974). *Use Your Head*. London: BBC Books.
3 See note 1.
4 Boardman, J. and Sauser, B. (2013). *Systemic Thinking*. Hoboken, NJ: Wiley.
5 See for example the Open University's Applied Systems Thinking in Practice; www.open.ac.uk/courses/choose/systemsthinking, accessed July 29, 2019.
6 Howard, R. A. and Matheson, J. (1981). Influence Diagrams, reprinted in Howard, R. A. and Matheson, J. (Eds.) (1984). *The Principles and Applications of Decision Analysis*, 2. Menlo Park, CA: Strategic Decisions Group, pp. 719–62.
7 Judea, P. (2005). Influence diagrams – Historical and personal perspectives. *Decision Analysis*, 2, pp. 232–34. Informs.
8 Ibid., p. 233.
9 Ackermann, F. and Eden, C. (2010). Strategic Options Development and Analysis, in Reynolds, Martin and Holwell, Sue (Eds.), *Systems Approaches to Managing Change: A Practical Guide*. London: Springer, p. 135.
10 Now available commercially as Banxia Decision Explorer.
11 Bryson, J. M., Ackerman, F., Eden, C. and Finn, C. B. (2004). *Visible Thinking: Unlocking Causal Mapping for Practical Business Results*. Chichester: John Wiley & Sons.
12 Senge, P. (2006). *The Fifth Discipline*. London: Random House.
13 Senge, P., Ross, R., Smith, B., Roberts, C. and Kleiner, R. (1994). *The Fifth Discipline Fieldbook*. London: Nicholas Brealey Publishing.
14 Jackson, M. (2003). *Systems Thinking: Creative Holism for Managers*. Chichester: Wiley, p. 80.
15 Sibbet, D. (2010). *Visual Meetings*. Hoboken, NJ: John Wiley & Sons.

Standards-based visuals

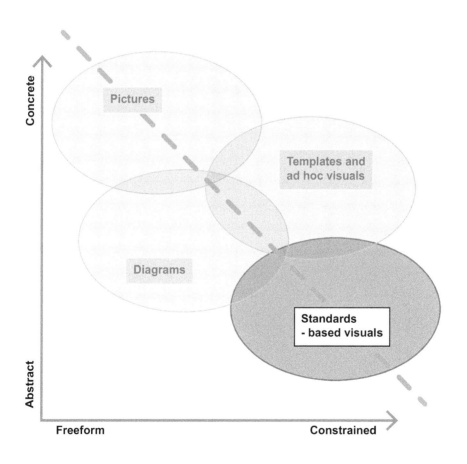

We now come to the end of our journey along the Visualisation Continuum. Standards-based models adhere to a set of rules that determine the elements that can appear on the models, the relationships between those elements and the notation used to visualise the elements and the relationships. The additional level of constraint arises from the fact that these rules are agreed not just by convention but by internationally agreed standards. In a sense, while the pictorial models at the other end of the Continuum attempt to create shared meaning by making the meanings explicit in the immediacy of the visuals used, standards-based models do so by making the meanings explicit in the written-down definitions. As some knowledge of the standards is often necessary to interpret standards-based visuals, we have included annotated versions of the examples in this chapter.

Foundations of standards-based visuals

Modelling standards

There are many standards[1] for modelling business change, many of which are 'open'. The Object Management Group® (OMG®)[2] is an international, open membership, not-for-profit technology standards consortium, founded in 1989. OMG standards are driven by vendors, end users, academic institutions and government agencies. OMG's modelling standards include the ISO-adopted Unified Modelling Language® (UML®) – we discuss UML in more detail later in the chapter in the section on software design diagrams – and the Business Process Model and Notation (BPMN). These standards enable visual design, execution and maintenance of business processes and computer software. A full list of the standards (and links to their associated specifications) published by the OMG is available on their website.[3]

Many in the 'people and change' community struggle to understand why technical experts are so inflexible in their use of diagramming approaches. They often fail to realise that, given how reliant the average large modern organisation is on technology, the importance of shared meaning is not restricted to human beings. Consider, for example, the development of Model Driven Architecture® (MDA). In essence, MDA is a forward-engineering approach to the development of software systems which starts with user-defined models such as UML Activity models and Class models and, through automated transformations (based on transformation patterns), produces executable system software – a sort of hands-free approach to software development through UML modelling. The potential benefits of the MDA approach are numerous and include: lower development costs; greater stakeholder engagement (as more of the effort is visual and front loaded); increased consistency; faster time-to-market and return on investment; improved architecture (as the representation of models as views on the architecture mean that the system architecture can relate directly to those models); clearer developer responsibilities; and improved agility.

MDA tries to span the range of human–machine interactions shown in Figure 7.1. The problem is that it cannot deal with the ambiguity that humans compute as an integral part of their daily lives and which they interpret through their experiences. Machines can talk to machines, but only if the interactions are defined explicitly – and despite the advances in machine learning.

It is rarely the case that from a set of user-defined models the resultant auto-generated code is complete for the context in which it is created. Often subsets of systems may be suitable for MDA. So, MDA rarely means that the creation of the solution is totally automated. The models are not experiential and the code is not complete, but the aspirations of MDA are understandable, at least in terms of the automation of software development.

Although many modelling standards are 'open' – i.e. their content is freely available with minimal restrictions to their usage – in reality they relate to a closed community. The UML specification, for example, points out that one of the language's goals is 'to advance the state of the industry by enabling object visual modelling [software] tool interoperability'[4] (which we discuss later in the chapter). However, to enable meaningful exchange of model information between tools, agreement on semantics and syntax is required.

Human ⟵⟶ Human   Human ⟵⟶ Machine   Machine ⟵⟶ Machine

Figure 7.1 Human and machine interactions

In the example in Figure 7.2 the arrow in the rich picture is open to interpretation – although given the notation, the context is some form of association between two people, e.g. B reports to A (in this case, the placement of A above B may suggest that), B passes work to A for approval, B informs A of an event, etc. In the case of the UML Class diagram, the triangular-headed arrow has a very specific meaning, namely 'generalisation' – suggesting that B 'is a type of' A.[5]

If they are to be machine-readable and capable of being interpreted by computer software, models need to be specific and with appropriate detail. The UML specification provides the required semantics and syntax (and notation). And therein lies the limitation of modelling standards: to really understand and model using the language, you need to be reasonably conversant with the standard, although you can interpret models with a basic knowledge of the notation. The notation is abstract: see, for example, the Use Case diagram in Figure 7.3, which represents user requirements (or more specifically, the interactions between an actor – which may be a human user or another system – and a system) with ovals.

The Rational Unified Process (RUP)[6] software development process introduced the concept of Business Use Cases (as distinct from system use cases), the latter being interactions between an actor and a business (where the business itself is a system). However, as shown by the example in Figure 7.4, from a visualisation perspective the only difference is the diagonal line on the business actor icon and the Business Use Case icon, and the reader would need to be told what the distinction means (UML itself makes no distinction between system use cases and Business Use Cases).

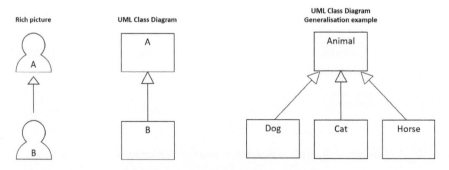

Figure 7.2 The meaning behind notation

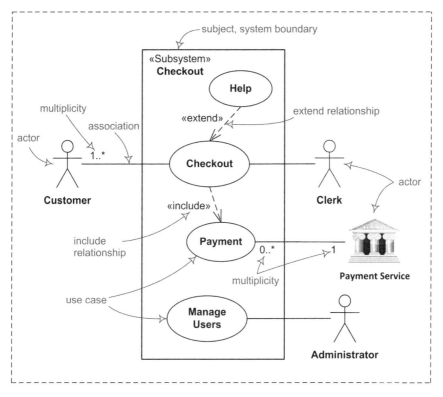

Figure 7.3 UML Use Case Diagram

Published with permission from uml-diagrams.org.

In general, the notation may be meaningful to the modeller, but what about the user? There is nothing inherent in the shape of an oval that reflects a user requirement. When the UML standard refers to 'the industry' (as quoted above), it is not explicit about which industry is being referred to, and although the implication is any industry, the reality is that in the context of object visual modelling tool interoperability, this is quite a specific community.

However, this is not a criticism of standards-based visuals or variants of them, but rather a characteristic of models that are intended to be interpreted by machines. Machines aren't bothered about the notation, they just need to know exactly how to interpret that notation. Humans, by contrast, are bothered by notation. A computer can be programmed to

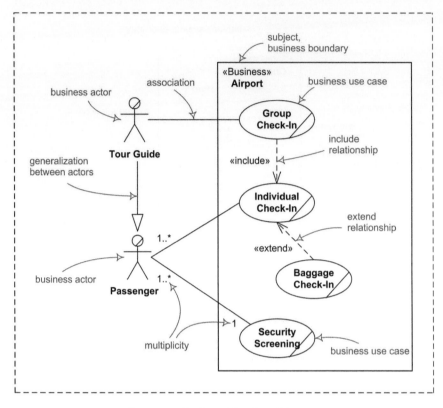

Figure 7.4 Business Use Case Diagram

Published with permission from uml-diagrams.org.

understand the UML specification, but a human needs to be convinced that it will be a worthwhile investment of time.

A perception of the use of modelling standards is that they ensure consistency of the models produced – each modeller uses the same concepts and notation to construct their model. However, the use of a notation doesn't mean that consistency and meaning is guaranteed – it just means that modellers are using the same concepts and notation! Each modeller may interpret the concepts in the notation differently; in BPMN, for example, there are processes, sub-processes and tasks, all of which are defined as types of Activity. But what one modeller interprets as a process, another may interpret as a sub-process, and when we rise from operational to strategic level, there are process concepts such as value streams and process chains which are not covered in BPMN. The level of abstraction leaves it open to interpretation.

Modelling is about perspective, and one modeller's perspective of a system may be quite different to another modeller's perspective. Even for a simple modelling assignment the range of possible models is considerable and it is rarely the case that two architects will create identical models.

There are many languages and diagrammatic standards, some of which are complementary and some of which are competing. BPMN, for example, competes with UML for business process modelling. If there are multiple change initiatives running in parallel in an organisation, you don't really want different standards being used when they are modelling similar things, not if you are expecting shared meaning across the organisation. But there are also some equivalent characteristics between the languages, enabling a natural transition from one language to another. For example, the ArchiMate Application Cooperation viewpoints can be modelled using UML Collaboration/Sequence diagrams.

Every language will have its compromises and is unlikely to be able to accurately represent the real world, which is itself far from unambiguous!

Frameworks, methodologies and bodies of knowledge

In Chapter 3, we mentioned change management methodologies and the point that each methodology comes with its own 'tool kit' – methods and techniques (and terminology) – and for standards-based visuals there are a plethora of such frameworks. ISO/IEC 42010[7] defines an architecture framework as: '*conventions, principles and practices for the description of architectures established within a specific domain of application and/or community of stakeholders*', a recognition that such frameworks (and their associated models) are not for everyone. The predominant frameworks are 'open', some are industry specific, or at least have their roots in a specific industry (e.g. DoDAF,[8] MODAF[9] and TRAK[10]) and others are universal (e.g. TOGAF®;[11] version 9.1 weighs in at over 750 pages). The website for the ISO standard ISO/IEC/IEEE 42010 'Systems and Software Engineering – Architecture Description' includes a list of over 70 architecture frameworks.[12]

Many organisations define, or adopt/adapt an existing open framework such as TOGAF, within which models are created. Many consultancies, industry analysts and architecture tools vendors also have frameworks, and many organisations use no framework at all.

Many of these frameworks have their roots in IT (and specifically technology infrastructure, that is, the tin and wire), but have evolved to cover software, data and information, business process and business capabilities. There are also frameworks that have emerged from a specific focus, for example the Enterprise Design Framework[13] (for enterprise strategic design) which we discuss further in Chapter 8 and the 4EM Method[14] (for enterprise modelling).

As well as frameworks, there are also other 'bodies of knowledge' that provide guidance on modelling (see, for example, the Business Analysis Body of Knowledge[15]), and these may define types of models that should be produced.

The Zachman Framework[16] (which is a classification scheme rather than a framework) provides an interesting way to model enterprises[17] and changes to subsets of enterprises and changes to enterprises, based on a 6 × 6 matrix, as shown in Figure 7.5.

Its columns are founded on the primitive interrogatives (what, how, when, who, where and why) and the rows represent different perspectives (which equates to different types of stakeholders, e.g. planners, designers, users) on those interrogatives, through reification – the progressive trans-formation from the abstract to concrete forms. Each cell of the matrix is a primitive viewpoint and combinations of cells are composite viewpoints (see the section on viewpoints and views later in the chapter). Interestingly (and intentionally), the Zachman Framework does not prescribe any spe-cific modelling notation for any of the viewpoints, leaving it to the modeller to determine what is most appropriate for them. Therefore, in terms of the Visualisation Continuum, the populated framework would equate to an idiosyncratic/taxonomical model as there is no standard set for the visuals contained within it. As an aside, some people may deduce that the framework is used to model entire enterprises; that is not the case, and would certainly be impractical today given the complexity and pace of change of organisations.

In terms of the paradigms we introduced in Chapter 3, it is probably fair to say that the frameworks that underpin standards-based models are the product of communities of people who see the world through a more deterministic paradigm, as opposed to those who tend to see the world emergently (such as change managers, systems thinkers and designers).

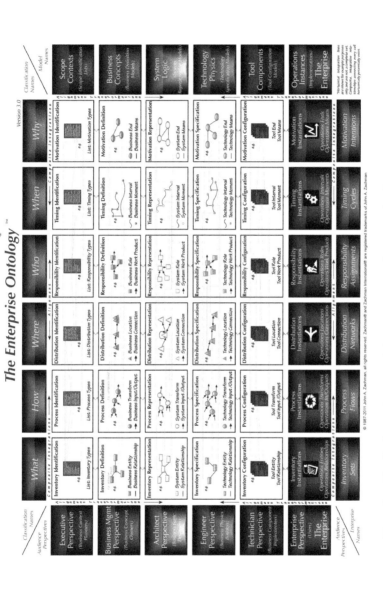

Figure 7.5 The Zachman Framework for enterprise architecture (for illustrative purposes only)
Published with permission from John A. Zachman, Zachman International®, Inc.

Consequently, shared meaning tends to be confined to the community who created the models, and others are generally excluded, not because the content is irrelevant to them but simply because they are not familiar with the conventions of the visual language.

Reference models

Reference models are readily available models that represent one or more aspects of the organisational system. Some reference models are industry-agnostic (such as the Business Motivation Model[18]), some are industry-specific (such as eTOM[19] for the telecommunications industry), some are discipline-specific (such as the Supply-Chain Operations Reference[20] or the COBIT[21] framework for the governance and management of enterprise IT shown in Figure 7.6) and some are organisation-specific (such as an organisation's proposed customer journey map). So, there is in effect a continuum of reference models from general purpose to organisation-specific, and many organisations will take an industry model and adapt it for their own specific purposes.

Reference models can provide a lot of value by, for example:

- Providing a standard way of defining elements of the organisation (e.g. processes, capabilities, information, etc.) and hence promoting stan-dardisation across organisation units, as well as partners, suppliers, customers and other industry participants;
- Helping to simplify the complexity of the organisational system by giving each unit a standard 'template' to work from; for example, when large organisations are striving to establish a consistent customer proposition, or eliminate the unnecessary duplication and process diversity that arises over time from organisational evolution, mergers and acquisitions;
- Providing a 'check-list' of elements to be considered when modelling change in a particular domain;
- Reducing time-to-market by reusing existing material and skills.

A key point of these models is that they should be a basis for shared meaning, with the people who consume them interpreting them in the same way. However, that very much depends on how they are represented and who the intended audience is. Reference models may be intended for

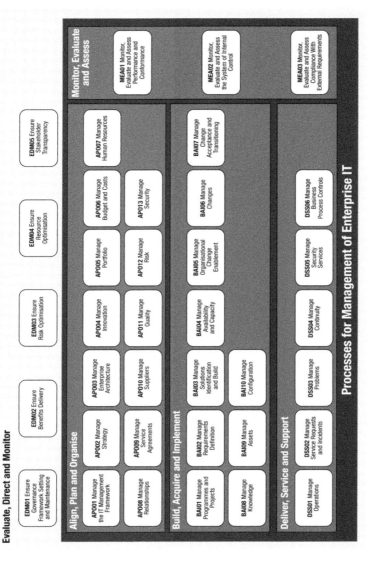

Figure 7.6 The COBIT framework
Published with permission from ISACA.[22]

the masses, but their visual representation may limit them to the 'chosen few'. Many organisations are striving for global standardisation, but without creating globally agreed and understood points of reference (or reference models); federation of capability across an organisation needs to be accompanied by good reference models, along with training and engagement to ensure that they are being interpreted in the same way.

Reference models allow organisations to easily (and cost-effectively) adopt best practice in areas of the business that do not generate strategic value, leaving more time to concentrate management attention on the areas that will deliver competitive advantage. There is no sound reason why an organisation would not want to adopt open standards in this way. Sooner or later, maintaining proprietary capability that is becoming commoditised in the marketplace will make no commercial sense: it will become a major impediment to the organisation.

Despite their name, reference models are certainly not a 'silver bullet' when it comes to creating shared meaning. Not all organisations are the same: their history, culture and other factors determine their unique characteristics. Not thinking enough about these characteristics and shoe-horning in a reference model (with concepts and terminology that stakeholders do not relate to) can cause more harm than good. However, there is no reason why these limitations cannot be avoided or overcome with effective communication, training and – where necessary – adaptation.

Metamodels

A metamodel is a model of the elements to be modelled – a model of a model. So, if a model is a diagrammatic representation of a system, a metamodel is a diagrammatic representation of the elements that are used to model that system, the relationships between those elements, and any rules (or constraints) regarding those elements and their relationships. If a model is an abstraction of phenomena in the real world, then a metamodel is yet another level of abstraction. Many modelling languages and frameworks are underpinned by a metamodel. And modelling repositories (see later in the chapter) that support standard frameworks and modelling languages 'out of the box' include the underlying metamodel associated with that notation, explicitly or implicitly, thereby enforcing the rules of the languages.

Probably the best way of describing a metamodel is to use an example. Figure 7.7 shows the metamodel of the core content of TOGAF.[23] It identifies those entities that relate to an enterprise (equivalent to an organisation in this context). Each element in the metamodel is associated with a definition: the idea is that every element in every model produced using the framework should link to a description of what kind of element it is, and what kind of attributes and relationships it can or should possess.

An organisation's metamodel can act as a Rosetta stone, particularly for large organisations, as it offers a common language between models created autonomously by individual divisions or domains. In principle, this should provide the basis for ensuring completeness and consistency of models, identifying gaps and overlaps, and enabling their extension in a co-ordinated way. Metamodels also provide the foundations for the interoperability of tooling software – see the section later in this chapter on tools and repositories for standards-based visuals.

However, metamodels are usually created as conceptual data models (see the section later in the chapter on entity-relationship models), so they tend to be visually very abstract, and therefore appeal to a relatively small community. This is a shame, given their power for reducing complexity and creating shared meaning. In one business we have been involved in, the metamodel made clear the distinction between the four elements at the bottom of Figure 7.7 (Data Entity, Application Component, Technology Component and Platform Service) by colour-coding them in a way that is consistent with the other elements in the model. Each element had a senior manager responsible for it, and each senior manager could see (visually, at least) their 'world' in relation to their peers, the associated responsibilities, and how each had a part to play in providing a business service.

We believe that metamodels are vastly underutilised when it comes to shared meaning, not helped by the notation used to create them. Surely, this should be a natural meeting point for people at the two ends of the Visualisation Continuum to develop metamodels that are more consistently meaningful to a broader range of users.

Types of standards-based visuals

There are a number of ways that we could categorise the various types of standards-based visuals. We could, for example, categorise models in line with

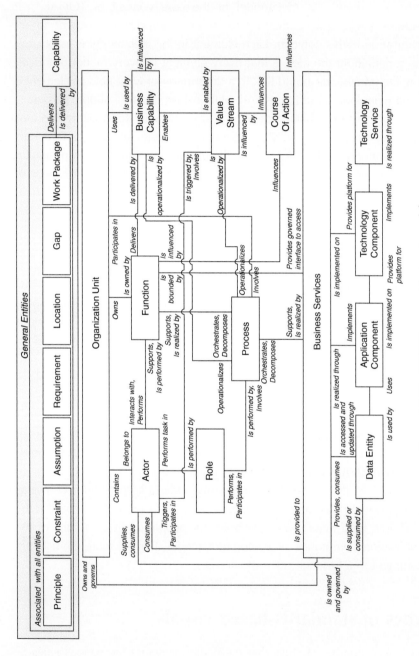

Figure 7.7 The TOGAF core content metamodel

© The Open Group. Published with permission from The Open Group.

the Systems Development Life Cycle (SDLC)[24] in which case we would describe domain models (models of the business domain to which the intended system relates), specification models (logical models of the software system itself and the interfaces with user tasks) and physical models (how the system is actually put together). However, if all of the models are produced using UML, then they are all at the bottom-right end of the Continuum. In contrast, an example of a visual showing an IT systems domain model unconstrained by a formal modelling standard is shown in Figure 6.2.

However, as the visuals in this chapter are based on standards produced by recognised standards bodies (and underpinned by their respective metamodels), the categorisation of the visuals is predefined by the standards' specifications – although extensions are possible in order to accommodate the needs of individual organisations.

In this section we survey four main types, with each one being broadly more abstract and constrained in its form (and therefore progressing down the Continuum). We make a distinction between the type of visual and the language on which the visual is based, focusing in each case on the type of visual.

As with the rest of the book, bear in mind that we are only including a representative sample of the most popular modelling languages in use.

Business process visuals

The most prominent standards-based business process visuals are those created using the BPMN, published by the OMG. The specification[25] states that:

> The primary goal of BPMN is to provide a language that is readily understandable by all business users, from the business analysts that create the initial drafts of the processes, to the technical developers responsible for implementing the technology that will perform those processes, and finally, to the business people who will manage and monitor those processes. Thus, BPMN creates a standardised bridge for the gap between the business process design and process implementation.

But what confirms the placement of BPMN-based models near the bottom-right of the Visualisation Continuum is the goal of the specification itself, namely:

127

To ensure that XML[26] languages designed for the execution of business processes, such as WSBPEL (Web Services Business Process Execution Language),[27] can be visualised with a business-oriented notation. This specification represents the amalgamation of best practices within the business modelling community to define the notation and semantics of Collaboration diagrams, Process diagrams, and Choreography diagrams. The intent of BPMN is to standardize a business process model and notation in the face of many different modelling notations and viewpoints. In doing so, BPMN will provide a simple means of communicating process information to other business users, process implementers, customers, and suppliers.[28]

It also goes on to say that:

A key element of BPMN is the choice of shapes and icons used for the graphical elements identified in this specification. The intent is to create a standard visual language that all process modellers will recognize and understand. An implementation that creates and displays BPMN Process Diagrams SHALL use the graphical elements, shapes, and markers illustrated in this specification.[29]

In other words: 'BPMN provides businesses with the capability of understanding their internal business procedures in a graphical notation and will give organizations the ability to communicate these procedures in a standard manner'.

Alternative modelling notations include activity diagrams in the Unified Modeling Language (see the later section on UML). BPMN is often the default choice of modellers whose focus is business processes, whereas UML activity diagrams are often the choice of software modellers. However, BPMN is the dominant player, reinforced by a comprehensive array of supporting resources; in addition to the BPMN specification (which is over 500 pages), there is a huge array of books, online materials, training courses and certifications available.

A simple, annotated BPMN diagram is shown in Figure 7.8.

There are also more than 40 extended BPMN modelling elements (each with an associated notation/symbol). There is a core structure that underpins the elements of BPMN set out in the specification (and visualised through a set of metamodels). In terms of BPMN diagram types, the

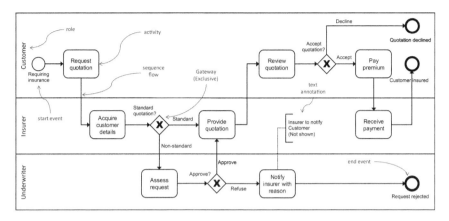

Figure 7.8 An example BPNM diagram

specification aims to cover three basic models of processes: Private Processes (both executable and non-executable), Public Processes and Choreographies – which in itself suggest some knowledge of the specification being essential in order to produce models compliant with the standard. Within and between these three BPMN sub-models, many types of diagrams can be created.

The more you want to do with process models, the more you need to understand the standard. For most users, a modest notation of a symbol to represent a process and arrowed lines to represent process flow is sufficient for shared meaning between humans. The more complex the model (in terms of the variety of element types used – each with its own notation), the fewer people will relate to it. A key to shared meaning is to be specific but without unnecessary detail. If you want a machine to read and correctly interpret (even with the best artificial intelligence) a process model, you need the specificity that comes with a modelling standard.

In terms of meaning to humans, greater success is likely when adopting language that the people actually performing the process will understand. Arguably, the reason why so many businesses undertake one-off process mapping initiatives, where the models end up on the shelf rather than being maintained, is that the people who perform the processes do not relate to the models. Perhaps if there were more meaningful ways of modelling the processes, they would have greater longevity, and hence the potential for a greater return on the investment in them.

Entity-relationship models

'In God we trust, all others must bring data.'[30] 'Data is the new oil.'[31] 'Torture the data, and it will confess to anything.'[32] There are many such aphorisms that speak to the criticality of data and information to the modern organisation;[33] models of that data and information are often referred to as entity-relationship (ER) models or diagrams.

We live in an era dominated by digitisation and communication, and information is at the heart of it. As individuals, we rely on it in our day-to-day lives and for most organisations it is their lifeblood. Information covers every aspect of an organisation, including its customers (and their behaviours, preferences and experiences), its products and services, and the operations and assets that create, deliver and maintain those products and services. And, because of its importance, organisations need to adapt to manage and exploit it. But when it comes to visualising data in *business* transformation, it remains largely elusive. It seems reasonable to assume that when visualising business change, information models and data models would be prominent. However, the reality is that they tend to appear in pockets, and most often when designing computer systems; they are usually thought of as being mysterious, with only the anointed few – the data modellers – able to truly understand the value of them. Data modelling is, to many people, abstract, but understanding the data needs of a business change is imperative.

ER models represent the data captured, stored, managed, processed, shared and reported by organisations. A significant percentage of ER models are produced using UML Class models and Object models[34] or Barker's notation.[35] Traditionally they have come in three general types: conceptual, logical and physical.

Conceptual data models (CDMs) – sometimes referred to as domain data models or subject area data models – model the key business entities (the things that the organisation needs to know about) and the relationships between those entities. It is a data model of the business, not business systems and is therefore independent of software applications, technology infrastructure and operational procedures. In theory, therefore, these models should be experiential, but in reality (and because they are underpinned by a modelling notation) they are abstract. Figure 7.9 is an example of a conceptual data model for a customer sales domain in Barker notation; the diagram has been annotated to explain the notation. Shared meaning is

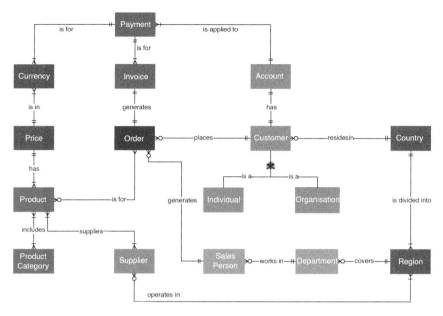

Figure 7.9 Conceptual data model

possible as the model does not adopt a formal notation other than identify-ing entities and relationships. Note the use of colour to distinguish related types of entity (product related, currency related, etc.). Contrast this domain model to the example UML domain model in Figure 7.14.

Logical data models (LDMs) (Figure 7.10) model the entities, relation-ships and their attributes – the data that will actually be stored and maintained; they must, therefore, define the entities with more rigour. The logical models are storage and technology agnostic, and do not depict the actual physical representation of entities. The logical model guides the physical realisation of a model. In terms of shared meaning, LDMs provide more detail in the form of text, defining attributes of the entities and thereby making their definition more specific, and giving more meaning to the relationships between entities.

Physical data models (PDMs) represent the physical realisation of the entities, relationships and attributes applied within physical data stores (databases, files, etc.). The physical data model should be aligned to the logical data model. Shared meaning at this level is, understandably, limited to those that need to know – solution designers, data store designers, etc.

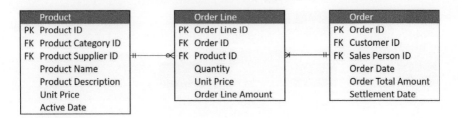

Figure 7.10 Logical data model

Whilst PDMs provide an accurate representation of how data are to be stored, visually there is little difference to LDMs.

In the hierarchy of CDM → LDM → PDM, each model 'informs' the model below it, and each model is (or at least should be) traceable to the model above it. Going from CDM to LDM is, in data terms, a journey from the abstract towards concrete, but visually, other than the addition of the text, there is little difference.

Cardinality (or multiplicity) provides additional information about the relationships between entities. For example, in Figure 7.9, the relationship between a payment and an account is that a payment is applied to one (and only one) account, and conversely an account may have zero or more payments applied to it. Cardinality equates to business rules, and so can be a powerful construct in data models and the modelling of business change. Cardinality is shown visually using numbers or symbols (depending on the notation) at the end of relationships between entities; in Figure 7.9 it is the Barker notation that we mentioned earlier which is used. It is probably fair to say that the notation is not exactly intuitive.

The level of data model to use depends on the audience and the context. For example, for modellers (or anyone for that matter) wanting to understand the domain of change, then CDMs are ideal. For analysts participating in the development of a new software system, or making changes to an existing one, then an LDM is important. And for systems developers, data store administrators, etc. who are maintaining data stores and assessing the impact of change, then PDMs are a must. A simple conceptual model of, say, the 10–15 key information entities (and the relationships between them) on an A4 page, with concise, specific descriptions can be a potent way to promote a common language across the organisation and to promote shared meaning.

Enterprise architecture diagrams

These visuals are based on enterprise architecture (EA) modelling standards, most notably the open standard ArchiMate,[36] although other proprietary languages exist. Whilst architectures (including all their variants: business, data, applications, technology, security, etc.) can also be modelled using other languages (e.g. UML/SysML for solution architectures), these other languages are not devoted to architecture modelling.

According to the ArchiMate specification,[37] ArchiMate is

> a visual language with a set of default iconography for describing, analysing, and communicating many concerns of Enterprise Architectures as they change over time. The standard provides a set of entities and relationships with their corresponding iconography for the representation of Architecture Descriptions.

Three core layers are defined, one for each of the business, applications and technology environments:

- The *business layer* offers products and services to external customers, which are realised in the organisation by business processes performed by business actors;
- The *application layer* supports the business layer with application services which are realised by (software) applications;
- The *technology layer* offers infrastructure services (e.g. processing, storage, and communication services) needed to run applications, realised by computer and communication hardware and system software.

Each layer provides capability for the layer above it. So, the application layer provides capability to support the business layer – e.g. application services are *used by* business processes, and technology services are *used* by application components. Each of the layers has a metamodel which explicitly describes the elements of the layer (more about these later) and relationships between them. Note that there is no data layer. This is because data are treated as being passive and so have no capability to support the layers.

Figure 7.11 shows an example of the ArchiMate language; it demonstrates how the language can be used to model an architecture, end to end, from the user through to the technology infrastructure, in this case for an insurance claim.

ArchiMate (as well as TOGAF and many other architecture frameworks) gives the perception, both textually and visually, that layers are built on top of each other, i.e. applications on top of technology, and business processes, roles, etc. on top of applications, perhaps reflecting its roots in IT.

In terms of the types of diagram that can be created, the standard does not prescribe a specific set. Instead, it provides a set of example viewpoints (see later in this chapter for more about viewpoints), although this doesn't stop users creating their own.

Software design diagrams

These visuals are usually even more abstract and constrained than the preceding types. Most examples are based on UML, and the less common SysML. Interestingly, UML is underpinned by object orientation, from the field of object-oriented programming (OOP) which emerged in the late 1980s and into the 1990s, a key tenet of which was to make system structures map more cleanly onto the real-world structures that they represent. A number of approaches to software design existed for the modelling of such structures, and those approaches were 'unified' by three systems practitioners, James Rumbaugh, Ivar Jacobson and Grady Booch, to form the Unified Modeling Language (UML),[38] which was adopted by the OMG, with the UML specification[39] being initially published in 1997. UML rapidly became a standard notation for modelling software-intensive systems and is now encapsulated into the ISO/IEC 19505 standards.[40]

The UML specification states that 'one of the primary goals of UML is to advance the state of the industry by enabling object visual modelling tool interoperability. However, to enable meaningful exchange of model information between tools, agreement on semantics and syntax is required.'[41] The specification, which is almost 800 pages long, provides the required semantics and syntax. UML is, as the name *Unified* Modeling Language indicates, one diagramming standard, incorporating many diagram types. It is aimed at the software development community and so the main

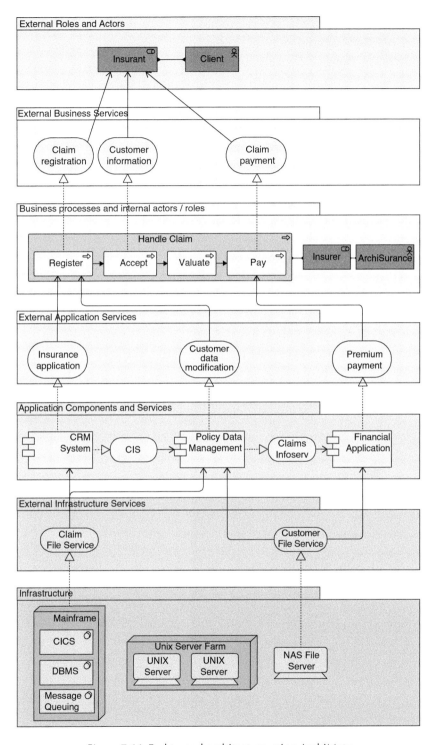

Figure 7.11 End-to-end architecture using ArchiMate

© *The Open Group. Published with permission from The Open Group.*

stakeholders are business analysts and software development stakeholders (solution architects, systems engineers, etc.). Creating and interpreting UML diagrams clearly requires a thorough understanding of the specification, but this is not necessarily an easy thing to acquire from the specification itself. After a decade using UML, software engineer Kirill Fakhroutdinov created a website[42] for his own reference, including annotated examples, to make the specification more interpretable. At the time of writing, the site received almost two million visitors and four million page views per year (or over 450 page views every hour), indicating the need for it; the annotated UML diagrams included in this chapter are from the website.

UML defines a taxonomy of diagrams as shown in Figure 7.12, divided into two general types: Structure diagrams and Behaviour diagrams. Figure 7.12 is itself an example of a Structure diagram.

As with most standards-based models, there is a need for some explanation for those not 'in the know' to be able to make sense of this diagram. The lines here are *inheritance* lines, so each diagram type is a type (or *subtype* in UML terms) of the diagram that it points to. So, for example, a Sequence diagram is a type of Interaction diagram and an Interaction diagram is a type of Behaviour diagram. A Behaviour diagram is a type of Diagram (at the top of the tree). The diagram equates to a visualisation of a taxonomy. The types of relationship that exist between model elements

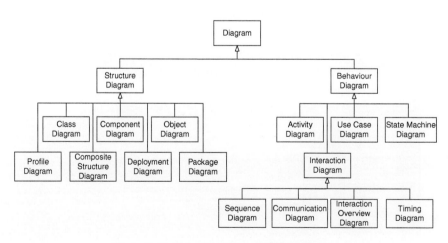

Figure 7.12 The taxonomy of UML diagrams

are constrained by the types of element being related; it is the language's metamodel that determines which relationship types can be applied to relate various element types.

Structure diagrams tend to focus on the elements of the organisation that are relatively static, and although of course these elements do change, the emphasis is on how they are organised and relate to one another. For example, they include *Component models* as a broad categorisation of models (see the example in Figure 7.13). They are common in engineering, in particular software engineering, where they are used to model applications and technology infrastructure. The UML specification defines a component as 'a modular unit with well-defined Interfaces that is replaceable within its environment.' It goes on to say that 'the Component concept addresses the area of component-based development and component-based system structuring, where a Component is modelled throughout the development life cycle and successively refined into deployment and run-time'.[43]

Component modelling is a good way of showing reuse of existing components, whereby new systems can be created and reinvigorated by assembling and adding existing components rather than creating new ones from scratch, or creating monolithic structures that are complex and inflexible. *Product models* (where in retail *product* is merchandise and in manufacturing it is items bought as raw materials and sold as finished goods) could be viewed as a type of Component model.

Another example of a Structure diagram is a Class diagram (Figure 7.14[44]). Classes[45] equate to entities in ER diagrams. The use of UML introduces constructs (and associated notation) that need to be understood, such as *aggregation* and *composition* and the distinction between them. Contrast this diagram to the less rigorous ER domain model in Figure 7.9.

Some attributes of the classes are shown in this example; at a conceptual level they are not necessary, but they can help to provide more explanation of the model. Note, for example, the distinction between a Book and Book Item, the latter of which is an instance of the Book and is uniquely identifiable by the RFID (radio-frequency identification, shown as an attribute). Behaviour diagrams focus on the more dynamic aspects of the business – that is, the 'how' of the system, and how those behaviours need to change.

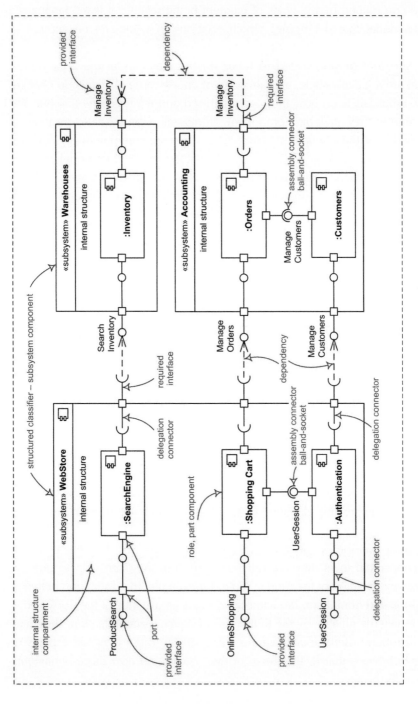

Figure 7.13 UML component diagram
Published with permission from uml-diagrams.org.

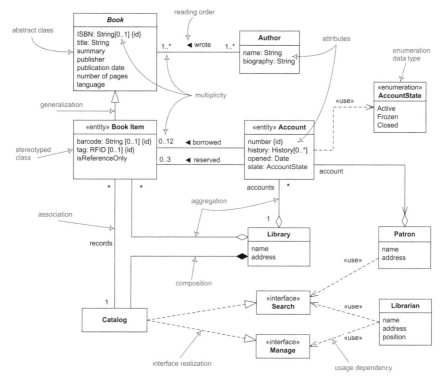

Figure 7.14 UML Class diagram – domain model diagram

Published with permission from uml-diagrams.org.

Figure 7.15 shows a UML Communication diagram, which shows the interaction elements.

Without knowing the language, visually the only significant thing is that Bookshop appears to be the primary element – it is the only element that connects to every other element. Determining the order in which things happen requires the reader to jump around the diagram to follow the sequence. Sequence diagrams (another UML Behaviour diagram) focus on the sequence of the interchange, and that sequencing is represented visually (see Figure 7.16) though once again the diagram requires specialist knowledge to understand. The general point here is that to outsiders these diagrams are not intuitive, and certainly not easy to read.

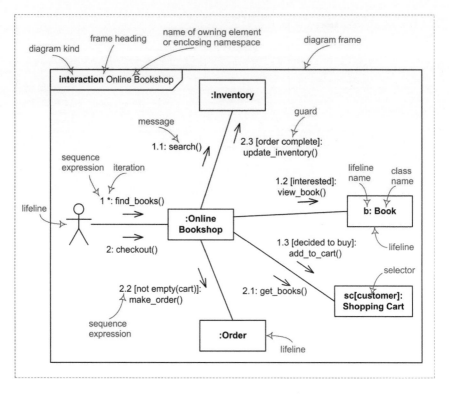

Figure 7.15 UML Communication diagram

Published with permission from uml-diagrams.org.

Further insights into standards-based visuals

Shared meaning vs accuracy

This brief review of standards-based visuals highlights the trade-off between achieving shared meaning and accuracy (or specificity). Standards-based models, by their very nature, strive for accuracy, but at the expense of shared meaning – at least, shared meaning among humans. We represent it as a trade-off; with current methodologies and tools it's very hard to have it both ways (although we very much hope that you will join us in challenging this state of affairs, a journey that we begin in Part III of this book).

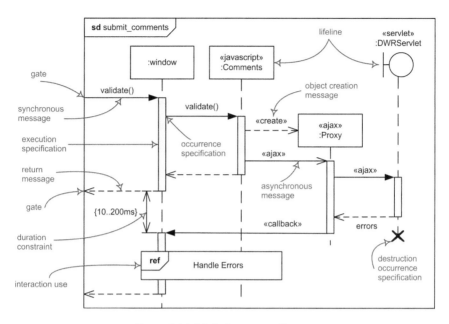

Figure 7.16 UML Sequence diagram

Published with permission from uml-diagrams.org.

As we said in Chapter 1, many (human) users are generally excluded from standards-based models, simply because they are not familiar with the conventions of the visual language, and the basics cannot be taught rapidly enough for them to be able to follow along productively. Given that most standards-based visuals have their roots in IT, it is the non-technical users who are excluded. This can be a significant inhibitor for transformation programmes striving for seamless, efficient change.

But when it comes to machines, shared meaning is achieved only through accuracy, or more specifically, explicit definition – there is no room for misinterpretation if you want to avoid the inevitable 'Error' message (unless of course the explicit definition is wrong).

Viewpoints and views

Too often we see visuals that try to answer all the questions of all the stakeholders; a creative mix of structured and freeform concepts, large dollops of colour and a sprinkling of invisible magic dust intended to make the model meaningful for everyone. The result is invariably an A3 diagram, often sized down to A4 so that it fits into a presentation deck. It's a disaster waiting to happen. As Manfred Eigen stated, 'A theory has only the alternative of being right or wrong. A model has a third possibility: it may be right, but irrelevant.'[46] Overwhelming stakeholders with irrelevant detail is likely to alienate them and switch them off. Equally, not presenting them with enough information will leave them cold. It is also important to consider the natural tendencies and circumstances of the stakeholders and to use their language and their metaphors. For the stakeholders that have to transform the architecture into a business design, it is essential to include all the information necessary to achieve the desired transformation without loss or misinterpretation. Consequently, the same information has to be presented differently to parties of different interests. How that balance is achieved is a matter of experience, whether in the modeller's head or codified into procedures and guidance.

The German physicist Max Planck is attributed to saying, 'When you change the way you look at things, the things you look at change'. As human beings we see the world from different perspectives, and these perspectives are influenced by our goals and interests as well as our values and beliefs. The significance of perspectives is foundational to virtually all of the systems approaches to change and modelling that we looked at in the previous chapter, and in enterprise architecture this significance has been codified in the form of viewpoints and views. These increase the probability of shared meaning by producing visuals focused for specific audiences, rather than a 'one size fits all'. The concept originates from the field of computer system development and the work of Finkelstein.[47] The complexity associated with modelling software systems was recognised as involving many people who each have their own perspective on the systems, influenced by their skills, knowledge and experiences, and each describing and visualising the systems from their perspective. The challenge is to optimise not just the co-ordination of these people but also the models that represent their perspectives, so that there is shared meaning as well as shared goals. But the concept is not confined to the bottom right of the Continuum; customer journeys and rich pictures (in the original Soft Systems Methodology sense) are like single-person viewpoints. The concept of perspectives is critical to the communities at both ends of the Continuum:

- A *viewpoint* is a definition of the perspective from which a view is taken. It is a specification of the conventions for constructing and using a view (often by means of an appropriate schema or template);
- A *view* is what is seen from a viewpoint, when the viewpoint has been populated with real content. Although a view doesn't have to be a visual representation (it could be text or a matrix, for example) in this book we focus on visual representations.

Primitive viewpoints are constructed using only a single type of model element, such as business processes, locations, business assets, technology assets, etc. As these are representations of individual elements and the relationships between those elements, they are by their nature simple models, thereby (in theory at least) increasing the potential for shared meaning. A simple process flow is an example of a model based on a primitive viewpoint. Models based on primitive viewpoints are particularly useful when defining scope, impact analysis and as reference models.

In contrast, *composite viewpoints* are constructed using many types of model element, often resulting in complex models, and thereby decreasing the potential for shared meaning. Most models are composite models, not because they need to be but rather because the modeller has not made a conscious decision on which type of model to produce. Many technical modellers have a tendency to try and cover all bases in one model, rather than by producing several simpler, related models. That said, a simple composite model is often more meaningful than a primitive model.

The entities in the metamodel represent the most granular elements from which viewpoints can be constructed – used on a single entity for primitive viewpoints and two or more entities for composite viewpoints. A metamodel acts as a palette that can be used to 'drag and drop' (literally, if using a modelling tool) into models. This can make it easier to ensure consistency.

Based on their roots in the deterministic community, and by their very nature highly structured, viewpoints are typically associated with visuals at the bottom right of the Continuum. Viewpoints appear in many modelling languages, frameworks and methodologies, including (to name but two): ArchiMate 3.0[48] (and ArchiMate 2.1[49] for example diagrams) and TOGAF.[50] The Business Analysis Body of Knowledge (BABOK®) Guide[51] uses the concept of 'perspectives'. And in the field of software development, Philippe Kruchten proposed the '4+1' view model[52] for describing the architecture of software-intensive systems.

Viewpoints and views have nevertheless evolved from focusing on software and technology to cover all the elements of an organisation; creating personas in product design and user experience modelling is analogous to the identification of stakeholders for which viewpoints are to be created. The Business Model Canvas (see Figure 5.11), for example, equates to a viewpoint.

The layers in ArchiMate and in many of the architecture frameworks are examples of viewpoints. Additional viewpoints can be defined that relate to views that are orthogonal to the layers, such as a security viewpoint which links the security-related aspects of each architecture layer.

Clear separation (sometimes referred to as 'separation of concerns' or 'loose coupling') between layers and elements within the same layer, makes it easier to address individual elements independently of the others – a divide and conquer approach to understanding what is impacted and what needs to change.

And, as mentioned earlier, technology prejudice is arguably manifesting in the fact that the architecture layers are always built from technology up and not the other way around.

Model overlays

Whilst model overlays are not specific to standards-based visuals, they are often used on such visuals and so we include them here.

Models are an investment and, like any investment, you want to maximise the return on it. Model overlays are one such way. Overlays are often used with formal models, especially enterprise-level models such as business capability models, value chains, locations models and information models, and they represent effective usage of those models, especially those which already carry shared meaning.

Overlays are particularly good for giving a high-level view of the status of elements of organisations, primarily because of the (enterprise-level) models that they overlay. For example, a business capability model can be overlaid with the operational cost of each capability, and/or the proposed investment in each for the next financial period. Alternatively, a process model could be overlaid with timings, customer satisfaction ratings, number of executions in the last reporting period, etc. Overlays that use a RAG (Red, Amber, Green) or GAP (Good/Adequate/Poor) assessment are often referred to as heat maps.

Figure 7.17 shows a business capability model with a simple overlay showing the coverage of an Enterprise Resource Planning application on the organisation's capabilities.

Although overlays are more common in standards-based visuals, their concept is equally applicable, and arguably, more valuable in conveying a message in freeform models, given how much closer their representation tends to be to people's experiences.

Model patterns

Patterns have their origins in the architecture of buildings (and specifically in the work of Christopher Alexander[53]), where it was recognised that different projects incorporated many of the same problems, and that generic solutions could be applied to similar problems.

In its most general sense, a pattern is a recurring form or arrangement of elements. It is the result of experience of having solved the same problem many times (and learned from the shortcomings of earlier solutions), and so provides a solution to a known problem. So, a pattern is a solution to a problem that exists in a specific context.

Patterns have an important role to play in society – in the architecture of buildings, mathematics, statistics, geometry, language, process and soft-ware design – and patterns in business can be found wherever reuse of design is sought. Patterns can also be useful when visualising business change. A pattern captures the information necessary to successfully apply design on a repeated and rapid basis. The real value in patterns is that they capture and codify 'know how' so that it can be referenced, reapplied, modified and evolved many times over. Patterns require discipline to develop and document, but once they are developed and tested they become packages of wisdom that may even turn out to be patentable.

Figure 7.18 shows a simple visual example of a 'Request Form Approval' process pattern[54] as implemented in a BPMN model. The goal of a 'Request Form Approval' pattern is to perform management approval for data entered earlier on a form, earlier in the same workflow. Examples of form-based approvals include employee requests, such as a vacation request or a travel authorisation. A 'Request Form Approval' works when

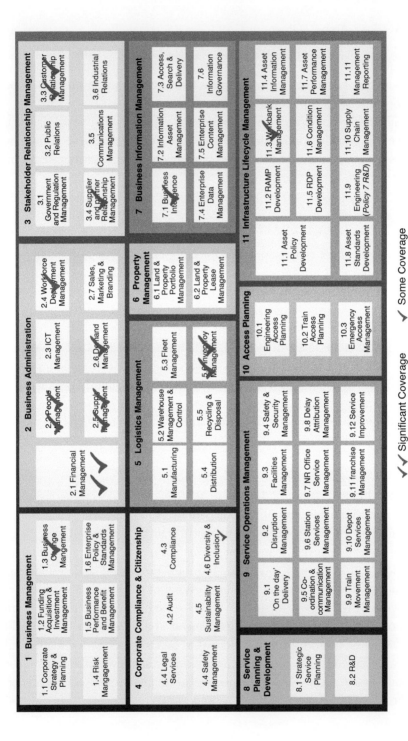

✓✓ Significant Coverage   ✓ Some Coverage

Figure 7.17 Simple overlay on a business capability model

Reproduced with permission from Network Rail.

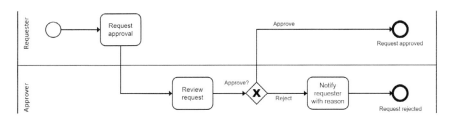

Figure 7.18 'Request Form Approval' process pattern

all of the information about the request can be captured in a single form, so that the information required for the decision is captured as part of the workflow.

This version of the pattern assumes that a decision to reject the request cannot be resolved by changing the request. An alternative would be to add a task to change the request so it can be approved.

While the concept of patterns tends to be associated only with the technical implementation side of business change, this is a concept that deserves to be understood and embraced on a much broader scale.

An example of an innovative application of the concept of patterns to the strategic discussions that trigger business transformation is Hoverstadt and Loh's work on 'Patterns of Strategy',[55] in which the authors offer 80 strategic patterns, built from simpler archetypes of how organisations can be structurally coupled to their environments. Each pattern is visually represented almost as a kind of 'play' in the longer-term game.

Tools and repositories for standards-based visuals

It's important that we discuss tooling (i.e. the software tools used to create and maintain models) here, because to produce models that conform to a standard requires discipline. Many of the tools[56] that are used to create standards-based visuals come with the notation and rules built-in, and may include functionality to support the subsequent utilisation of those models in an automated or semi-automated way such as the auto-generation of computer software code, etc. Such tools can constrain and validate the creation of standards-based visuals and, like the standards that underpin them, they are often only accessible to a few specialists.

In general, the more formal the model and the modelling environment, the more comprehensive the associated tools tend to be. At the top left of the Visualisation Continuum, for example, live artwork requires no more than pen and paper, and rich pictures tend to be built using either traditional media or digital illustration packages. However, at the more formal bottom right of the Continuum, features may include:

- Support for a range of model languages (not just their notations but also their rules);
- A repository to store and manage along with the ability to partition models and work collaboratively in a multi-user environment;
- A metamodel to provide the specification required to structure (or program) the tool and the elements of the models that will be created;
- One or more frameworks/methodologies to provide a structure for the models to be produced;
- A catalogue of viewpoints out of the box and the ability to create new ones;
- (For software development) support for Model Driven Architecture as a software design approach for the development of software systems;
- Reverse engineering and round-trip engineering;
- The ability to create roadmaps;
- Simulation;
- The ability to merge and compare models.

Supporting features include interoperability (providing the ability to share models, metadata, taxonomies, catalogues, etc. with other modelling tools) and integration with the tools of other disciplines such as portfolio management.

The challenge of trying to construct a single diagram that is technically correct, visually pleasing, exec-friendly, etc. etc. is ... impossible! There is unlikely to be one diagram/model that meets the needs at all levels and at all stages of the change lifecycle. So, inevitably there is a trade-off between the freedom to create freeform models and the ability to subsequently codify the models – e.g. to generate executable code from those models.

However, in many situations the need for a specialist tool becomes increasingly apparent. Tooling is useful in a static situation but really comes into its own in the context of a change initiative, when current- and future-state models are under development and fluid. During this period, without such tooling, much time can be wasted maintaining duplicated data in the models. Using a modelling tool, information can be captured once and then reused many times without the overheads of duplication. And a tool with structured, well-managed content can be an invaluable single source of the truth as the initiative progresses. Integration with other tools and repositories is common, enabling, for example, foundation models to be imported thus increasing the consistency of modelling within the organisation.

Tools can also create a collaborative environment. Models stored in a central repository can be viewed, revised and enhanced by those with appropriate permissions to do so – something which is especially beneficial in dynamic, fast-paced, global environments where modelling may be distributed across geographies and time zones. Nevertheless, as we have been saying throughout this chapter, shared meaning still tends to be limited to those who know the standard and have access to the tool.

Describing change shouldn't have to be a specialist activity, practised by the chosen few. The fewer people describing change, the narrower the perspectives, the less likelihood of innovation and the greater the risk of misunderstanding, especially in larger organisations. In fact, the risk is probably proportionate to the size (number of people) in the organisation … including agents of the organisation (consultancies commissioned to implement a change – who may themselves come with their own language and models).

Notes

1 Documents approved by a recognised body, that provides, for common and repeated use, rules, guidelines or characteristics for products, processes or services with which compliance is not mandatory (ISO 9453).
2 www.omg.org, accessed July 29, 2019.
3 www.omg.org/spec, accessed July 29, 2019.
4 UML specification – http://www.omg.org/spec/UML/, accessed July 29, 2019.
5 Generalisation is a fundamental and, in many respects, complex construct in UML and beyond the scope of this book. Refer to the UML specification for further details.
6 Kruchten, P. (1998). *The Rational Unified Process: An Introduction*. Boston, MA: Addison-Wesley.
7 ISO/IEC 42010 – originally IEEE Std 1471:2000 – *Recommended Practice for Architectural Description of Software-intensive Systems*, www.iso-architecture.org/ieee-1471/index.html, accessed July 29, 2019.
8 http://dodcio.defense.gov/, accessed July 29, 2019.

9 www.gov.uk/guidance/mod-architecture-framework, accessed July 29, 2019.

10 https://sourceforge.net/projects/trak/, accessed July 29, 2019.

11 TOGAF is a registered trademark of The Open Group.

12 www.iso-architecture.org/ieee-1471/afs/frameworks-table.html, accessed July 29, 2019.

13 Guenther, M. (2013). *Intersection*. Amsterdam: Elsevier/Morgan Kufmann.

14 Sandkuhl, K., Stirna, J., Persson, A. and Wißotzki, M. (2014). *Enterprise Modeling: Tackling Business Challenges with the 4EM Method*. Heidelberg: Springer.

15 www.iiba.org/standards-and-resources/babok/, accessed July 29, 2019.

16 www.zachman.com, accessed July 29, 2019.

17 An enterprise is the highest level (typically) of description of an organisation and typically covers all missions and functions. An enterprise will often span multiple organisations (TOGAF).

18 www.businessrulesgroup.org/bmm.shtml.

19 Business Process Framework (eTOM) by the TM Forum, www.tmforum.org.

20 The Supply Chain Operations Reference (SCOR®), http://supply-chain.org/scor.

21 www.isaca.org/cobit/pages/default.aspx.

22 COBIT 5®, ISACA, https://cobitonline.isaca.org/, accessed July 29, 2019. All rights reserved. Used with permission.

23 http://pubs.opengroup.org/architecture/togaf9-doc/arch/, accessed July 29, 2019.

24 A process for planning, analysing, developing, testing and deploying software systems.

25 Version 2.0, www.omg.org/spec/BPMN/2.0/, accessed July 29, 2019.

26 Extensible Markup Language; see www.w3.org/XML/, accessed July 29, 2019.

27 See www.oasis-open.org/committees/tc_home.php?wg_abbrev=wsbpel, accessed July 29, 2019.

28 Version 2.0, www.omg.org/spec/BPMN/2.0/, accessed July 29, 2019.

29 Ibid.

30 Attributed to W. Edwards Deming.

31 Attributed to Clive Humby.

32 Attributed to Ronald Coase; www.coase.org/aboutronaldcoase.htm, accessed July 29, 2019.

33 Here we use the terms 'data' and 'information' synonymously, although we recognise (and data aficionados may insist) that there is a clear distinction between them, namely that data are raw facts and information is data that has a meaning (in a context).

34 See the UML specification for more information about Classes and Objects – www.omg.org/spec/UML/, accessed July 29, 2019.

35 Barker, R. (1990). *CASE Method: Entity Relationship Modelling*. Reading, MA: Addison-Wesley Professional.

36 ArchiMate is a registered trademark of The Open Group.

37 See http://pubs.opengroup.org/architecture/archimate3-doc/toc.html, accessed July 29, 2019.

38 Rumbaugh, J., Jacobson, I. and Booch, G. (1998). *The Unified Modeling Language Reference Manual*. Reading: Addison Wesley.

39 Version 2.5, www.omg.org/spec/UML/2.5/PDF/, accessed July 29, 2019.

40 See www.iso.org/home.html, accessed July 29, 2019.

41 UML specification – http://www.omg.org/spec/UML/, accessed July 29, 2019.

42 www.uml-diagrams.org/, accessed July 29, 2019.

43 UML specification – http://www.omg.org/spec/UML/, accessed July 29, 2019.

44 Whether Figure 7.14 is, strictly speaking, a conceptual model or logical model is beyond the scope of this book.

45 Strictly speaking, in UML terms, a Class is a classifier which describes a set of objects that share the same features, constraints and semantics (meaning).

46 Eigen, M. (2013). *Handbook of Organizational Economics*. Princeton, NJ: Princeton University Press.

47 Finkelstein, A., Kramer, J., Nuseibeh, B., Finkelstein, L. and Goedicke, M. (1992). Viewpoints: A framework for integrating multiple perspectives in system development. *International Journal of Software Engineering and Knowledge Engineering*, 2(1), pp. 31–58, March 1992, World Scientific Publishing Co. https://pdfs.semanticscholar.org/e9da/9abb38e581ef2823f8c3d60722f21911df8f.pdf, accessed July 29, 2019.

48 See http://pubs.opengroup.org/architecture/archimate3-doc/toc.html, accessed July 29, 2019.

49 See https://pubs.opengroup.org/architecture/archimate2-doc/, accessed July 29, 2019.

50 See http://pubs.opengroup.org/architecture/togaf9-doc/arch/, accessed July 29, 2019.

51 www.iiba.org/babok-guide.aspx, accessed July 29, 2019.

52 Kruchten, P. (1995). Architectural blueprints – The '4+1' view model of software architecture. *IEEE Software*, 12(6), www.cs.ubc.ca/~gregor/teaching/papers/4+1view-architecture.pdf, accessed July 29, 2019.

53 Alexander, C. (1977). *A Pattern Language: Towns, Buildings, Construction*. New York: Oxford University Press, and Alexander, C. (1979). *The Timeless Way of Building*. New York: Oxford University Press.

54 Source: Peter Hilton. See https://irmuk.co.uk/blog/business-process-modelling-patterns/, accessed July 29, 2019.

55 Hoverstadt, P. and Loh, L. (2017). *Patterns of Strategy*. Florence: Taylor & Francis.

56 Spending a few minutes on a web search engine usually brings up a range of results that list, compare and contrast structured modelling tools, usually categorised as enterprise architecture tools, software modelling tools, UML tools and so on.

Part III

Pursuing shared meaning

Finding shared meaning in models

Moving beyond boxes and lines

David Krakauer, President of the Santa Fe Institute for complexity research, said the following in conversation with Sam Harris:

> For a long time, psychologists, cognitive scientists, archaeologists, have understood that there are objects in the world that allow us to do things you couldn't do otherwise. A fork, or a scythe, or a wheel. But there is a special kind of object in the world that not only does what the wheel and the scythe and the fork do, but also changes the wiring of your brain so that you can build in your mind a virtual fork, or a virtual scythe, or a virtual wheel.[1]

Krakauer calls these objects 'complementary cognitive artefacts', and gives several examples – armillary spheres, astrolabes, sextants, quadrants, abaci. But the example he speaks most fondly of, and the one most familiar to the rest of us, is the humble map:

> Maps are a beautiful example of this. Let's imagine we don't know how to get around a city. Over the course of centuries or decades or years, many people contribute to the drawing of a very accurate map. But if you sit down and pore over it, you can memorize the whole damn thing. And you now have in your mind's eye what it took thousands of people thousands of years to construct. You've changed the internal wiring of your brain, in a very real sense, to encode spatial relations in the world that you could never have directly experienced. That's a beautiful complementary cognitive artefact.[2]

A map, of course, is just a specialised form of a visual model. The visual models we make of business exist for the same reason – they 'change the wiring of our brains'. What would it be like if, just as the maps that are made of towns are made for a broad audience, we could make models of businesses that all employees could understand? Is it possible that organisational models that took thousands of people thousands of man-years to complete, could be understood and appear in a similar way to the bulk of the workforce?

This is the question we address in this chapter.

The challenge, of course, is that a business does not exist in the same way that a city does. Organisational concepts and capabilities do not physically exist, so there is bound to be a much greater degree of variation in what kinds of maps make sense to different groups of people. Different communities have their own languages and preferred modelling techniques, which empower those familiar with them but ostracise those who aren't: it's usually only those with an IT or engineering background, for example, who are familiar with the conventions of UML. Organisation-wide change requires the building of understanding and consensus across organisational silos, so we have to find ways to build shared meaning without assuming that everyone has the same technical modelling literacy.

As we said at the start of the book, what we are really looking for are ways to align the *mental models* of disparate communities around the change that is happening. In other words, we are looking for ways to create *shared meaning*.

In this chapter we look at domains where this has been achieved already, then consider the implications for visual modelling in business. We have already mentioned one such domain – cartography. The majority of people can use a geographical map to find their way around a location without needing a degree in map-reading. We will now go on to look at marketing, architecture and engineering, each time considering how the modelling approaches have allowed potentially complex ideas to be represented in a way that generates shared meaning.

This makes it sound like the challenge is purely a technical one, when it clearly isn't. It's not just that different business constituencies use different languages because they have different technical requirements, but also because the languages become an expression of identity in their own right. Software engineers employ formal languages that are inaccessible to those not trained in them, but this barrier can become a marker of identity to delineate those who are inside and outside of the group, even if unintentionally. Graphic designers want to create visual models that are simple and beautiful not just because they communicate more clearly, but because they give them a sense of personal pride. Internal communications teams add business jargon to their presentation slide models not necessarily because the words have inherent meaning, but because they echo the language of those with power.

We could go on! This is not a book on social psychology, but we have to recognise that for most people in organisations, group identity, power relationships, professional pride and countless other non-technical factors have at least as big an influence on their use of language (even if only at a subconscious level) as the substantive meaning of the words they use. The same is true for models. When the everyday language of business is abstract and fragmented, it's easy for different groups to use the visual language of their preferred slides, templates or modelling techniques which thereby become badges of identity, regardless of their intelligibility, accuracy or usefulness – what's created for the group stays with the group!

How do we solve this problem? Clearly to answer this question fully would be well beyond the remit of this book. But as we seek inspiration from other domains, we will see that at least part of the answer is to create representations that speak to the *shared* experience and *shared* concerns of the communities being targeted.

Marketing: learning from the 'meaning industry'

As we said in Chapter 2, the word 'meaning' (and its equivalent in almost every language) has two primary senses:

- That we understand something (as in 'I see what this means'); and
- That it is important to us ('This means a lot to me').

So, in order to create shared meaning for a given audience, we need to connect to things that the audience not only understands but also cares about. How? As it happens, there is an entire industry dedicated to answering this question. The marketing industry (broadly defined) encompasses the inter-related disciplines of marketing, branding, advertising and PR, but all of these disciplines exist to align the mental models of customers with those of producers and (increasingly) to align the mental models of producers with those of target customers.

This is perhaps clearest with branding: the value of an organisation's 'brand' is the value of the *shared meaning* that the organisation and its products/services arouse in its target audience, so marketeers have developed a battery of techniques for influencing this meaning. As John Hegarty[3] said: 'Always remember: a brand is the most valuable piece of real estate in the world; a corner of someone's mind.' If we want to create visual models that catalyse and support change in our organisations, then we should pay heed.

Many people will treat this idea with suspicion, so to be clear, our attention here is not on learning techniques for 'selling' models, but for representing them such that they generate the same meaning for different people. They do this by connecting with experiences that are important to people, which is a lesson that we can all learn from.

Understanding the 'customer needs'

As is so often stated, marketing always starts with the needs of the customer; there is no way to create engagement with a target audience if you do not know what they care about. You can have the most accurate, elegant, powerful model, but if it does not speak to your stakeholders' concerns, they have no reason to engage with it.

When you are creating a model to discuss with an audience, it's useful to think how much of the model reflects your concerns, and how much reflects theirs. The focus of a meaningful discussion will be the overlap in the Venn diagram in Figure 8.1, so whatever the content of this overlap is, it should be reflected in the content of our model.

Creating experiences

Assuming you know what your audience cares about, the first and most powerful way to create shared meaning is not just to *connect* to associated experiences, but to create them directly. To use the marketing analogy, if we have a product we believe in, then the easiest way to validate it with customers is not to talk about its features, but to let them experience them.

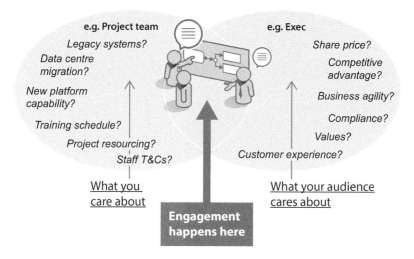

Figure 8.1 Meaningful discussion

Similarly, using props and real-life experiences brings models to life. For example:

- If your model speaks about user needs, record video of actual users articulating these needs to share as part of your presentation;
- If you are using a model to describe the reasons why an IT system is not working efficiently, have a live demonstration running on a laptop in the background;
- If you are describing the effects on customers of your current service architecture, invite an actual customer to the meeting to talk about what it feels like for them;
- If you are describing a wasteful or defective process, acquire some of the physical outputs of that process to use as props. John Kotter and Dan Cohen[4] give an example of a team acquiring a sample of each of the 424 kinds of basically identical gloves bought across a manufacturing business, and piling them complete with price tags on a board room table. The experience of actually touching price tags ranging from $5 to $17 across the huge pile had an enormous psychological effect, and procurement reform became an executive priority overnight.

These might not sound like models, but they are: in each case the experience itself is a simplification that stands for a more complex reality, allowing diverse groups of people to build shared meaning around what needs to change.

Telling stories

Psychologists describe stories as 'psychologically privileged'; in other words, the brain notices, understands and recalls information better when it is presented in narrative form. The art of creating, influencing and controlling stories is central to the art of public relations (PR), as corporate and political campaigns live and die by the stories that are relayed by the popular media. This fact has not been lost on internal business communicators, and there is now a whole ecosystem of experts, books, training and consultancy built up around the application of storytelling to the workplace.

This might seem antithetical to the whole idea of modelling, because models are typically built around the structure of the *system*, not the structure of a *narrative*, but to see this as a contradiction is to confuse how humans gather information with how they store it. Imagine you visit a new city and spend the day on a sequence of conducted walking tours. Each tour is a story, taking in new sites and experiences in a chronological sequence. After a while you spot the patterns across these stories and build an internal map in your head of where things are, based on repeated experiences of arriving at the same places.

This is equivalent to how PR campaign managers influence mental models. Each media story is like a tour around a city, taking in the highlights and avoiding the slums – the objective is to create a favourable mental model, not just to tell stories for their own sake. The stories are the hooks through which shared meaning is created.

Now contrast this to what it feels like to just look at a map of somewhere you've never visited and have no experience of. This is what it's like for an architect or a business analyst to talk through a model without using stories – it fails to connect to the audience's experience. It would be like a PR agent promoting a political candidate by running advertisements listing their virtues as adjectives. We don't believe politicians or companies or brands are honest or dishonest because someone says so, but because we read stories about how they actually behave in the real world.

Stories are relevant to modelling change on at least three levels. Firstly, at the lowest level, there are the stories that are implicit within the model – the user journeys, the process chains and value streams, the historical anecdotes and backstories implicit within the elements themselves. When marketing agencies design tourist maps for cities, they make sure that the main attractions stand out on the map, and provide clear itineraries for people to follow. Similarly, it's helpful when the main stories implicit in a model are made salient through the visual language – we will discuss this further below.

One suggestion for incorporating storytelling into architectural practice is to see everything in the enterprise as a kind of service, and each of these services as a story that culminates in the realisation of the enterprise vision:

> In effect, the vision represents the aim or purpose of the overall enterprise story; each value-flow is or represents another story within that greater story. To make sense of the enterprise, we describe it through *stories* of exchange and flow of value and added value.[5]

Each of these lower level stories has characters – suppliers and customers with their particular needs, desires and capabilities.

However, what is also required, and is present in all good stories, is the element of drama. Remember that meaning is as much about caring as understanding. What is at stake if any of the characters in these mini-stories should fail?

This takes us to the second level, which is that the enterprise itself is a story. All of the value flows work (or should work) together to serve some kind of greater purpose. This is the acme of attainment for all branding professionals: that the story of the brand that resonates with customers should be realised not just in the products and services that it sells, but also in its internal organisational behaviour.

Thirdly, there is the macro-story of the change affecting the organisation. If you have an 'as is', a 'to be' and perhaps some intermediate states, then you have already created an implicit story of change. Rich picture representations often draw this out. A chronological sequence, however, is only the very skeleton outline of a story. Why should people care?

Often what is missing from rich picture representations of change, is a sense of threat around what will happen if the transformation is not achieved. Stories work best when there is some form of antagonist to overcome, a threat to be resisted. There is no shortage of metaphors to depict this: running off the edge of a cliff as competitors build bridges to new technologies, becoming mired in a market that is becoming increasingly low margin,

Figure 8.2 Example transformation visual metaphor

and feeling the road crumbling beneath us as we try to innovate new solutions based on legacy platforms, as depicted in Figure 8.2.

We are now touching on the themes about metaphor and visualisation raised in Chapter 4 on rich pictures; it's surprising how often the power of visual language to tell compelling stories is short-changed by the unwillingness of management to be associated with 'negative imagery'. Yet stories that lack drama are not really stories, but merely lists of events.

The imperative of consistency

We said earlier that the value of an organisation's brand is the value of the shared meaning that it arouses in its target audience, and it is a sign of just how strongly humans associate meaning with visual symbols that for many people an organisation's brand and its logo are the same thing.

This leads us to our final, and perhaps most important, lesson from marketing: if a visual symbol encapsulates the meaning we want it to encapsulate for a given audience, then don't change it! When marketing departments initiate rebranding projects, they aren't (or shouldn't) be doing so because they are bored of the organisation's colour scheme – they are doing it because they want to shift market perception. If the market perception is where it needs to be then the branding doesn't change. The Coca Cola logo has barely changed in a hundred years.

Similarly with model making, once everyone understands the meaning of a particular diagram, icon, colour or label, then that meaning is an *asset* that the change programme can bank. It shouldn't be changed on a whim.

Interestingly, in our experience this can be the point at which these two worlds of branding and modelling come into conflict, because when a transformation team produces diagrams and pictures intended for communication and engagement, the internal communications team may see this as coming under their purview and insist that the visual language of the diagram be made brand compliant. When this happens, there will be an inevitable conflict between two sets of meanings:

- The meaning encapsulated in the internal branding guidelines, which is abstract and aspirational;
- The meaning encapsulated in the change diagram, which is grounded in the reality of the business's actual operating model.

So, for example, the branding guidelines might insist that any visuals should be photographic not diagrammatic, or restrict the palette to a small range of colours. Sometimes the colours will have meanings assigned to them (e.g. 'We use such-and-such shade of orange to convey the optimism of our brand promise'). These kinds of concepts simply don't translate easily into visual representations of operating models and the like, where the number of colours more likely reflects something intrinsic to the structure of the change (e.g. the number of top-level outcomes, service lines, departments affected, etc.).

This is an area worth further investigation, as although this chapter describes techniques for getting 'bottom-right' people to move up the Continuum by creating more shared meaning, there is equal onus for 'top-left' people to move down the Continuum by creating visual language that more accurately represents the reality on the ground. There is enormous opportunity here for those with a marketing and communications background: if they were to develop a fuller technical understanding of the business, could they not apply their skill in delivering consistent visual language to the conceptual world of the models supporting the transformation? It is not often that we have seen this being done, but imagine a set of consistently applied internal brand guidelines in which the visual language aligned, not just to the abstract aspirational qualities of the customer-facing brand, but to the actual structure, processes and everyday reality of the business. Brand reference banks would not just be filled with correctly formatted templates and banks of staged photographs, but sets of icons, symbols and images with consistent and specific meanings connected to the actual workings of the business. Changes to the business would then be reflected in updates to the visual language, so that what people see in their everyday lives and what they see in corporate communications would be in sync.

This may sound unrealistic, but the concept of a controlled visual language already exists at a much more abstract level in the various standards-defined modelling languages we explored in Chapter 7. A cube symbol will always represent a Node for anyone who is fluent in Archi-Mate. The trouble, as we have seen, is that it's meaningless to everyone else. Might there not be some way of combining the two approaches, i.e. building an internal visual language that has a maintained standard of consistency in the same way that formal modelling languages are controlled by international standards, but also creates shared meaning for its internal audience in the same way that the organisation's market-facing brand does for its external customers?

Architecture and engineering: creating digital counterparts

Most of the approaches we have described in this book assume that change is something that happens at a particular point in time, be that a small-scale agile software development project or a multi-year transformation programme, and the visual approaches are therefore a one-off collection designed to support that change.

Another approach would be to build a visual model of the current state and then keep it up to date as things change – a 'digital counterpart' that reflects the everyday operation of the organisation. The basic model could then be used to simulate potential changes and communicate desired future states. This has always been one of the main justifications for investing in enterprise architecture practices – by having a team maintain an underlying set of reference models, large-scale changes can be hypothesised and simulated using the models, rather than experimenting in real life.

The challenge, as we have said, is that these models are maintained in a format that is not meaningful to the rest of the organisation. Are there ways that this could be done that would create shared meaning? Are there ways that this is being done? This is what we will explore in this section.

Shearing layers and BIM

In 1994 Stewart Brand wrote an influential book called *How Buildings Learn*, based on studies he had made of the evolution of building use throughout their lifetime. In it he developed Frank Duffy's idea of 'shearing layers', elaborating how different aspects of the building evolve at different rates: at one extreme is the underlying *site*, which doesn't change at all, then at increasing levels of dynamism we have the *structure*, the *skin*, the *services*, the *service plan* and finally the *stuff* that fills the rooms (chairs, tables, lamps, pictures, etc.), which is continuously being moved around:

> Thinking about buildings in this time-laden way is very practical. As a designer you avoid such classic mistakes as solving a five-minute problem with a fifty-year solution, or vice versa. It legitimises the existence of different design skills – architects, service engineers, space planners, interior designers – all with their different agendas defined by this time scale. It means you invent building forms which are very adaptive.[6]

This concept from physical architecture has had a second lease of life in enterprise architecture, as a way to talk about organisational design, information system design and software development. Agile development teams, for example, need to be careful if they are making decisions at more fundamental shearing layers when they are designing entirely new solutions: one might develop the interface design for a web application based on rapid prototyping with users, but the underlying data model, server platform, not to mention the operating model of the organisation that sustains them, will all need to be designed with adaptation in mind, as they will be much costlier to change once implemented.

The question for us is, how can shared meaning be maintained across shearing layers? What kind of visual models can be generated to achieve this? One approach that has had a dramatic effect over the last decade on the design and construction of all physical infrastructure (not just buildings), is the concept of Building Information Modelling (BIM). BIM models are 3D models of physical assets/components where the key data about each component are embedded within the model – users can explore the construction in a 3D simulation, then simply click on the components to see their attributes (illustrated in Figure 8.3). The immediate benefits for

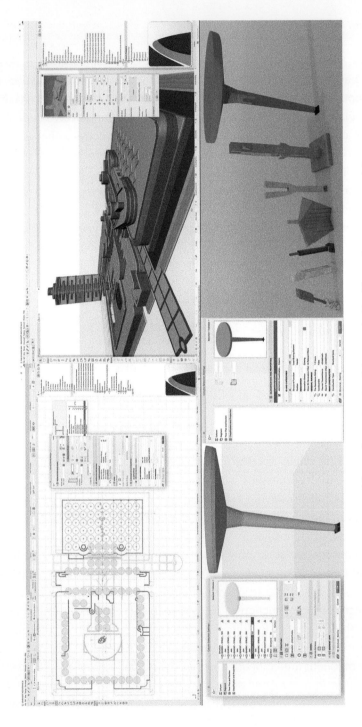

Figure 8.3 Building Information Model example (for illustrative purposes only)

Reproduced with permission from Graphisoft.[7]

BIM are in the short term, as the technology reduces friction in the design and construction process. It's much harder for different elements of a fragmented construction supply chain to misunderstand the design when everyone is accessing it through a shared data model and visualisation, and standard modules that work well can be reused over and over.

However, the potential benefits for BIM are much longer term. If 50 years from now someone wants to see how a building (or any other physical asset) could be repurposed, they could do so by querying the BIM model rather than performing physical investigations or experiments on the building itself. Of course, the building still has to be designed for adaptability, but the data in the BIM model will make this potential visible at a much lower cost. In Brand's terms, they are enabling agility at a lower shearing layer by giving transparency to the design of the underlying structure and services. The data become as much an asset as the physical asset itself.

BIM is a great example of what we describe as 'top-right' models in terms of the Visualisation Continuum: they have the technical accuracy and detail of an engineering schematic, but the concreteness of the 3D-rendered interface makes them meaningful to a general audience. Each component can be seen in the context of the overall building.

Applying this analogy to business change, how could we visualise businesses in a way that allows meaningful conversations at 'lower' shearing layers? While the purpose of physical assets can change markedly over time (e.g. the stately home becomes a military field headquarters, then a hospital, then a museum, then a conference centre, etc.), the change in organisations is much more significant. London Bridge (first built to span the River Thames in London) is now a tourist attraction in Nevada, but it still looks like a bridge. Nokia has had incarnations as a paper mill and as a rubber boot manufacturer in its 150-year lifespan – each of which would look completely different to its modern incarnation as a producer of networking technology.

Simon Wardley has developed a format for visualising this kind of change by mapping the different components of a business against (a) the value to the user and (b) its level of commoditisation, as shown in Figure 8.4.

This was Wardley's first map, of an online photo service he ran in 2005. He has since developed a whole set of insights and techniques based on this mapping format, and made them freely available online.[9] It's particularly

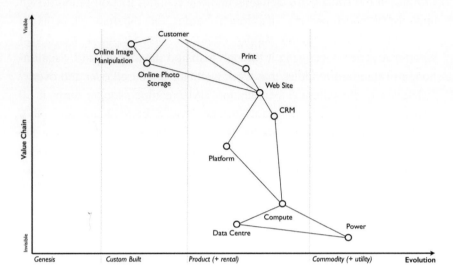

Figure 8.4 Wardley map

Reproduced under licence.[8]

interesting, in the context of this chapter, to note Wardley's description of what happened when he first created this map:

> For the first time in my business life I was able to have a conversation about what we thought was going to change without resorting to popular memes and hand-waving … we had a common language which we could use to discuss the future and collaborate over.

In other words, the maps created *shared meaning*.

Each map is a snapshot, but what is immediately apparent is their dynamic nature. They invite us to ponder what forces are pushing each of the components in different directions. They also give us a very simple way of looking at organisational components in terms of shearing layers. Elements in the bottom right are like the underlying structure in an architectural model: commoditised, with few pressures to change, but where any fundamental change would have serious ramifications on everything else, just as replacing the communications infrastructure at the 'services' shearing layer of a building with a completely new technology would require all the IT equipment to be upgraded as well.

Wardley maps are mainly used to support strategic conversations, so do not give a detailed view of the underlying architecture of each component (although the structure is recursive, so each component could be mapped in a similar way). The detail of these components will likely only exist in technical models and diagrams that only make sense to specialists in those areas, and are likely to be represented using standards-based models such as those in Chapter 7. Once again, we have the old trade-off between the detail required for technical accuracy and the simplicity required for conversations with shared meaning.

So where does this leave us? We have already mentioned in our review of advertising that shared meaning is created by connecting with shared experience. BIM achieves this by incorporating the technical data into the shared experience of three-dimensional space. People may not understand the architectural and engineering language used to describe each component, but they can at least see what the component is and where it fits, because we all have a shared experience of living life in a three-dimensional space. What could the equivalent of this shared space be in an organisational model? It would obviously need to be metaphorical, as organisations are conceptual constructs – they do not usually reside in a single physical space. Although Wardley maps are typically used more for strategic conversations than the detail of organisational design, we include them here as a great example of how that conceptual space could be constructed, relying as they do on conventional metaphors that connect with shared experience. Looking at the two dimensions, having 'value' as the Y axis is intuitive because we instinctively associate value with height ('more is better' is an in-built cognitive heuristic). Having the X axis as 'evolution' (i.e. maturity of the component) makes sense because we typically read time as a movement from side to side. As we will see in the next section, embedding conventional metaphors like these into visual models reduces the 'barriers to entry' for the audience, creating more shared meaning for more people.

We are still left with the problem, though, that when every element is represented as a dot with a label, most of the meaning is in the definition of the words, so we have to assume (or work to ensure) that everyone has a shared understanding of terms like (using Figure 8.4 as an example) 'CRM', 'Platform' and 'Compute'. Otherwise we are still only making meaning within the silo that uses those terms day to day. Are there other ways that we could build models that are still more visual, where the elements themselves look like the things they represent?

Digital twins

The concept of a 'digital twin' has been around for a while in manufacturing and engineering industries, particularly in the development of extremely complex/high-value assets such as airliners, military platforms and power stations. With the emerging wave of Internet of Things (IoT) technology, the concept has now become mainstream for a much broader range of organisations.

The BIM models we have just described sound like digital twins of buildings, but the term 'digital twin' is typically more associated with models that:

1   Link to onboard or environmental sensors that allow the product's real-time performance to be tracked, evaluated and modelled; and
2   Have the breadth and depth of data (e.g. mechanical, electrical, material, thermal, environmental, economic …) required to perform as close as possible to real-life simulations of the product or process.

These kinds of models and simulations can be used throughout the product lifecycle for a whole range of applications – design, user acceptance, real-time monitoring, maintenance, training and so on – and are increasingly integrated with other emerging technologies such as artificial intelligence and virtual/augmented reality. As a simple example, technicians can be trained for high-risk events in a virtual reality model of a plant that would be unsafe to simulate in real life.

What does this have to do with the process of organisational change? Well, many enterprise architecture tool vendors are rebranding their products under the label 'Digital Twin of the Organisation' or DTO. The twin forms by linking the organisation's operations (represented as a dynamic model, populated from, for example, monitoring systems) with other models such as a business process model or even its business model (i.e. static models) as a way of understanding its operations and exploring changes to those operations.

The first obvious point to make is that even in the manufacturing and engineering world, a 'digital twin' is not really a twin, it is a model. Real-life twins are typically identical counterparts, which means that they don't just have the same high-level information structure, but the same level of *complexity* (a twin sibling is a human being, not a simulation of a human being). To call a digital model a 'twin' is to mask the fact that a computer simulation can never have the same level of complexity as its real-life counterpart.

So if we accept 'twin' as marketing-speak for 'very similar', how similar does something need to be in order to be classified as a 'twin'? An aircraft engine has a finite number of components, which interact in a predictable way. A sophisticated model can therefore simulate the vast majority of circumstances that the engine could foreseeably be exposed to. In this sense the label seems apt – everything that is of interest in the real-life instance can be seen and modelled in the digital instance.

An organisation, on the other hand, is a complex adaptive system, not just a more complicated kind of thing. To re-visit the analogy from Chapter 3, working with an aircraft engine is akin to throwing a stone and seeing where it lands, whereas working with an organisation is more like throwing a bird and seeing where it flies. It is hard to escape the feeling that the rhetoric around DTO is inspired not by something fundamentally different about how organisations can or will be modelled, but by the marketing clout currently associated with digital twins, driven by the emergence into the mainstream of IoT and AI technology. We can certainly speculate about the effect of personalised data, improved performance tracking, smart analytics, etc. on organisational change, and data models that better reflect the way work actually takes place (as opposed to the way things get reported through the management chain) are going to have a substantial effect on the quality of operational decision-making, driving down cycle times and boosting process efficiency.

The question for us though is, to what extent will these technologies influence higher-level decisions around strategy, cross-organisational capabilities and large-scale transformation? Clearly plant operators can use digital twins of industrial processes to make far better informed asset management decisions, but what is the equivalent for a managing director pondering change to an entire operating model? The answer, as with our discussion contrasting BIM models and Wardley maps, surely depends on the extent to which the aggregate data and high-level trends can be expressed in a form that has shared meaning at executive level. A digital twin of an aircraft may be complicated, but at least everyone has the same basic understanding of what an aircraft is, so knows what they are looking at when they interrogate the model. People's mental models of what an organisation is, on the other hand, can be wildly divergent. If the visual model of the organisation remains a series of boxes, arrows and bar charts, the meaning is likely to carry on diverging. The closest the current generation of enterprise architecture models get to a shared framework for the entire business seems to be to include the ubiquitous Business Model Canvas template so that the rest of the model can be wired into it.

We already saw in Wardley maps the importance of context to meaning in strategic discussions. For shared meaning to be possible, the model needs to be represented using dimensions that people are already familiar with. We are not aware of any work being done to explore in detail how the visual language could work to create shared meaning at the macro level, i.e. how an entire operating model works. But we can speculate as to what it would involve. Connecting to shared experience means that the visualisation would preferably show what the work people do actually looks like – the raw materials, the tools, the activities, the locations, the interactions and so on – just as the digital twin of the engine actually looks like an engine. With the advances in simulation technology, this seems plausible, but would still require an overarching framework that was intuitive to people, just as exploring a 3D space is an intuitive way to understand physical asset systems.

Figure 8.5 is an early example of a map created by Steve's company Visual Meaning a few years back showing a high-level operating model of the European Union.[10]

The difference between this and a regular rich picture of an operating model is that this was built using interactive technology so that users could 'zoom in' on different parts of the organisation to see how they worked, just like in an online geographical map, as shown in Figure 8.6.[11]

When this approach has been used with client organisations, data has been embedded in the model, similar to BIM, showing how many people work in each department, providing descriptions of their activities, contact details and so on. The model can then be used to enable strategic conversations about the current vs the future model, and kept up to date to reflect the current state over the duration of the transformation.

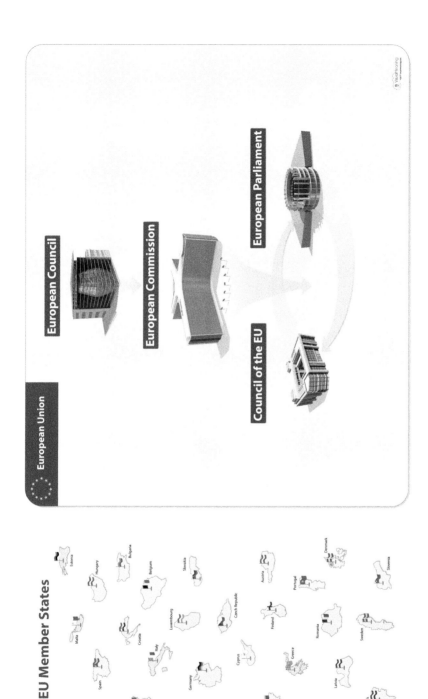

Figure 8.5 Operating model of the European Union

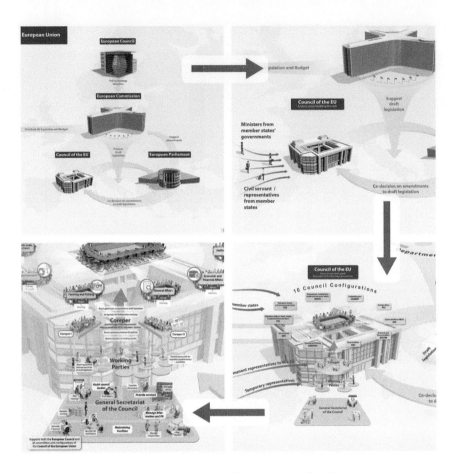

Figure 8.6 Zoomed-in detail of the Council of the EU

Although most of the imagery was created and maintained manually using studio-based design software, we include this as an example of what future enterprise architecture tooling could achieve using modern visualisation technology. The challenge, though, is not so much in finding meaningful ways to visualise the individual components, but in creating the conceptual space in which the relationships between those components make sense to a broad audience. As we mentioned when we discussed viewpoints (in Chapter 7), there is no single viewpoint from which everything can be modelled and everything can be seen – every viewpoint is a compromise.

So, this is a very tough challenge. There are, however, universal principles of cognition and visual language that could be applied in the development of these approaches, which would make shared meaning a more likely outcome. We turn to these now.

Levels of abstraction

Visual abstraction

In this brief examination of the use of visual language in other disciplines, we have stated that shared meaning is created by connecting with *shared experiences*. What do we mean by this?

We spoke at the start of the book about the significance of mental models in organisational change, and of how no two people have identical mental models. At the start of this chapter we described meaning as having two poles – the sense of 'do I understand?' and 'do I care?' Putting it all together, we can think of 'meaning' as what it feels like when there is a resonance between what we are paying attention to in the world and our mental models of the world. Good models close the gap between the two. We understand and we care, because the information is presented in a way that is familiar, that connects with our experience of what's important to us. When the same model is connecting with the same class of experiences for different people, then shared meaning is being created.

Many of our examples from marketing show that the main secret to achieving this is to ensure that the *forms of representation* are as close to the shared experience as possible, whether that be through consistent iconography, examples or stories. The same is true for visualising organisational structure. To illustrate this, look at the example of a Value Stream Map in Figure 8.7, a common type of model used to illustrate workflows that we have not mentioned previously in the book.

Value Stream Mapping has evolved a standardised set of not just diagrammatic but pictorial forms in order to convey meaning, which are commonly supplemented using iconography available in popular diagramming tools. Figure 8.8 shows the same model simplified so that every element is an identical box. Consider how much longer it takes to read and understand the same content.

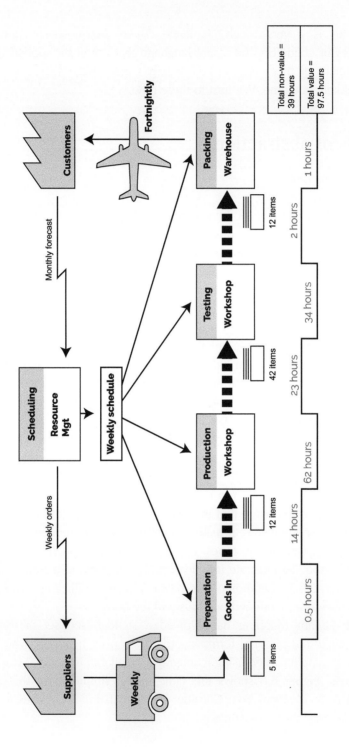

Figure 8.7 Example Value Stream Map – experiential representation

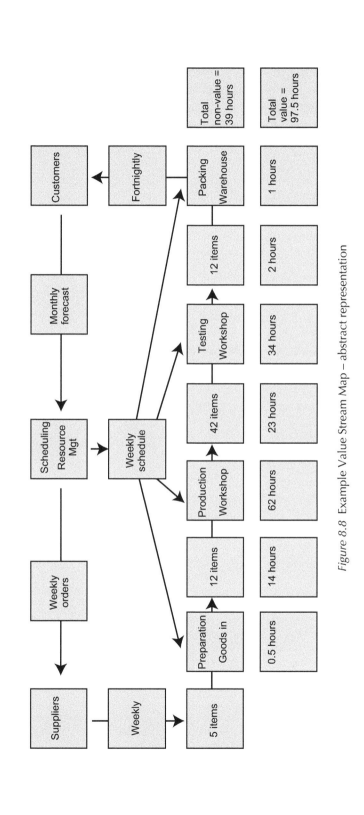

Figure 8.8 Example Value Stream Map – abstract representation

The important thing here is not so much that Figure 8.7 can be read more quickly, but that it is more likely to be interpreted in the same way by diverse audiences. This is because the form of the elements more closely resembles the *experience* of those elements as encoded in the mental models of disparate audiences: the production area *looks like* a factory, air transportation *looks like* a plane.

Compare this to the visual language (shown in Figure 8.9) of the most common process modelling language, BPMN, and again imagine the diagram without any of the icons.

The visual language of BPMN is restricted; it has to be because so many of the audiences for these models are machines, not humans. The point is that where we want to create shared meaning across a human audience, the further the visual form of content moves from shared human experiences, the less likely it is to mean the same thing to different people.

Abstraction ladders and the cost of shared meaning

Zooming out from diagrams, we can generalise this principle across all communication forms as a 'ladder' of abstraction. Visualisation has costs as well as benefits, and these abstraction ladders turn out to be a great tool for thinking about how this balance should play out when investing in models for change.

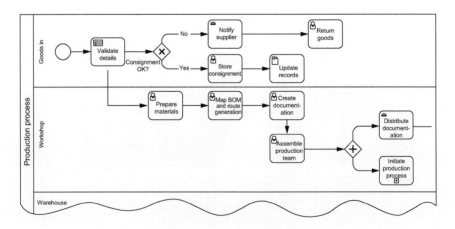

Figure 8.9 A BPMN example

A number of such ladder models have been created to illustrate the phenomenon of abstraction in general. The diagram in Figure 8.10 is adapted from an illustration used by Hayakawa[12] in 1939, which uses farm animals to illustrate the point.

Each level of abstraction takes us further away from tangible experience – we can experience 'Bessie the cow', but 'cow' in the abstract is a label for a pattern of experience. Nevertheless, each concept is articulated in the same form (i.e. a word or set of words).

When considering visualisation, we apply the same principle not just to the content of the communication but to the *form*, which gives us a ladder something like the example in Figure 8.11.

As with Hayakawa's ladder, the physical experience is at the bottom. The most effective way to communicate a concept is to show a real-life example of it. Which elements belong on the rungs above experience and whereabouts they fall are open to debate, and most visual communications (infographics, branding, iconography, rich pictures, etc.) will be a blend of the different levels.

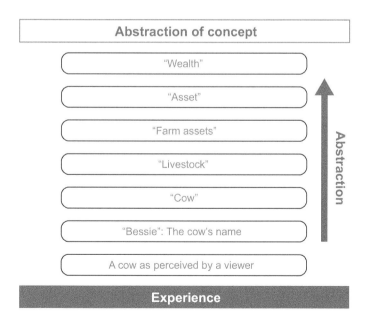

Figure 8.10 Abstraction of concepts

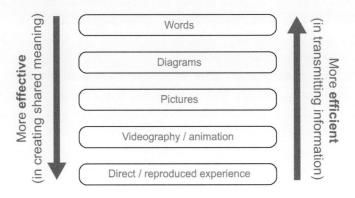

Figure 8.11 Abstraction of forms

Now look at the arrows on the side of the ladder. This diagram isn't meant as an exhaustive or scientific list of communication forms, but to observe that there is always a trade-off between the efficiency of a communication, in terms of how much information can be conveyed quickly, and its effectiveness, in terms of how much shared meaning is created. At the bottom are communication forms that are very similar (or identical) to the experiences of the concepts they represent, and at the top they have no resemblance whatsoever – their meaning is an arbitrary convention among a social group. There is nothing in the physical appearance (or spoken sound) of the word 'customer' that resembles anything to do with customers.

Another way to look at the ladder is as a representation of how communication evolves within a silo. Take as an example silo a specialist surgical team working in a hospital. When performing an operation, the team will be working at the top of the ladder, using technical words that convey a huge amount of information in an incredibly short space of time. This is essential – there's no time to stop and draw a picture when a patient is under anaesthetic. A medical student, on the other hand, has to spend years examining cadavers, watching videos of past procedures, cross-referencing against illustrations in medical textbooks, for any of this language to mean anything. In other words, they need to climb the ladder for each concept they encounter, and in so doing build a mesh of inter-related mental models that ultimately connect either directly or metaphorically to their personal experience. Eventually they will be able to perform live surgery as part of the team, but only because the technical terms the team uses have meaning built on years of study and practice.

Put this in the context of the Visualisation Continuum. The surgical team is operating in the bottom-right of the Continuum. Each team member has 'climbed the ladder': they can use the same words to mean the same things, and this shared meaning gives them agility within their domain. The surgical team, for example, can change the nature of a procedure halfway through if what they encounter is different to what they expect, but this is only possible because their shared vocabulary gives them instantaneous access to a huge level of shared meaning.

The challenge is, when most of the meaning in the organisation is 'trapped' inside individual silos like this, the agility that each domain possesses can count for nothing because the organisation as a whole is unresponsive. How does the surgical team respond when the entire hospital has its funding cut? Or an IT problem affects the availability of patient data? Or a legal suit threatens the reputation of the whole institution? Just as an individual silo can only respond adaptively when there is sufficient shared meaning within their silo, the organisation as a whole can only respond when there is shared meaning *across* silos. When representatives of each discipline meet together to respond to a shared problem, what language do they use?

These are the factors that need to be considered when deciding where to invest in visualisation. For which concepts does the organisation need to have shared meaning *across* silos, in order for adaptation and transformation to be possible?

We could argue that the reason visualisation has become such an integral part of organisational change is that diagrams and pictures represent a 'sweet spot' in the centre of the ladder, where efficiency and effectiveness balance out. Certainly, researchers in education have known for a long time that pictures and text in combination produce a marked improvement in learning outcomes over text alone. The graphs in Figure 8.12 are from Mayer (2001),[13] and show the result of a series of research projects he had led in the previous decade.

The graphs illustrate the percentage of correct answers students gave when tested on information that had been presented with or without illustrations. This is a result that has been replicated many times – the idea that visualisation boosts shared meaning is scientifically robust.

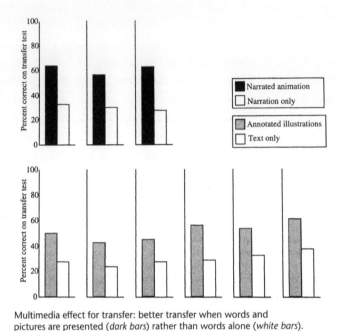

Multimedia effect for transfer: better transfer when words and pictures are presented (*dark bars*) rather than words alone (*white bars*).

Figure 8.12 Learning from words and pictures
Reproduced with permission from Cambridge University Press.

What the abstraction ladder points out though is that this shared meaning comes *at a cost*: someone had to make all those animations and illustrations! It's not that one end of the ladder is right and the other is wrong, but about learning to weigh up whether the *value* of the shared meaning is worth the *cost* of creating it. Imagine, for example, you are going to make a fundamental change to a key process that will directly impact customer experience, and it's going to affect your entire customer-facing workforce. Simply e-mailing everyone a BPMN diagram the day before the change would be highly cost-effective, but possibly disastrous! To create shared *meaning* about what's going to change so that you can be confident everyone at least *knows* what they are supposed to do, you'll probably need to invest significantly in videos, visual guides, simulations, trial days and so on, which will be costly but effective. In other words, you'll need to descend the ladder. Figure 8.11 helps to illustrate *why* these elements are effective: because they are using symbols that connect more directly to people's experience.

Looking at shared meaning as a targeted investment in this way, we should also recognise that there is a cultural as well as a financial cost. When a bridge of shared meaning is built between two cultural silos so that it becomes very hard for them to carry on ignoring or 'creatively misunderstanding' each other, the results can be unpredictable. Unspoken or unresolved tensions can rise to the surface, where they need to be carefully managed and resolved. This takes time and skill, which has to be factored into the investment decision.

In our experience, this is one of the big issues affecting rich picture engagement initiatives (which we discussed in Chapter 4): Leaders see the investment as starting and ending with the production of the picture and the opportunity cost of employees attending the sessions. They don't immediately think, for example, about the need to train facilitators in managing the emotional space that arises when colleagues from different backgrounds connect with the reality of what's going on around them.

User experience design

User experience (UX) design covers every aspect of a user's interaction with a product or service, from the initial acquisition, through usage to disposal. Don Norman, one of the founding figures in the UX movement, has described it as a form of systems thinking:

> No product is an island. A product is more than the product. It is a cohesive, integrated set of experiences. Think through all of the stages of a product or service – from initial intentions through final reflections, from first usage to help, service, and maintenance. Make them all work together seamlessly. That's systems thinking.[14]

User experience, conceived broadly in this way, overlaps heavily with the broader conception of marketing that we looked at in the previous section. We described the value of an organisation's 'brand' as the value of the *shared meaning* that the organisation and its products/services arouse in its target market. The whole point of UX design is to ensure that the promise of the brand – the shared meaning it evokes – is actually realised in the end-to-end customer experience.

That's the theory. In practice, UX design is almost entirely devoted to technology-based products and services, especially user interface design; behind the modern jargon, a huge number of those who now call themselves UX designers are people who once called themselves web designers.

The challenge that they face, though, perfectly parallels our challenge of bridging the top left and the bottom right of the Continuum, the top left being users, product owners representing users and those making brand promises to users, and the bottom right being the software developers who actually build the underlying product or service. Here are two of the fundamental principles that UX designers abide by that we can learn from in our pursuit of shared meaning:

- Don't make the user think;
- Understand user goals.

Let's take a closer look at each of these.

Don't make the user think

At the time of writing, the go-to exemplar for the broad conception of user experience is Apple Inc., which has topped the chart of the world's most valuable brands[15] for the past five years. Ask a branding expert why this is the case and they will probably talk about brand values such as individuality, self-realisation, creativity and so on. Ask dedicated users and they will often say that the products 'just work'. The real reason of course is the combination of the two: the products and services are designed to not get in the way of people doing what they want to do.

This is the primary lesson we want to draw from the world of UX and apply to visual modelling: the product has to do what the audience expects it to do. For example, the original iPhone was most people's first experience of a multi-touch interface, yet hardly anyone had to be taught how to pinch and expand to zoom in and out of a map, because it intuitively accorded with how we use our hands to shrink and expand things; children seem to do it instinctively. Usability expert Steve Krug summed up this imperative in the title of his first book, *Don't Make Me Think*.[16]

What makes an interface something people don't have to think about? A lot of the answer is bound up in the theory of abstraction that we covered earlier in the chapter. The closer an interface's form is to everyday experience, the less we have to think about it. If everyone knows how to move a piece of paper around a physical desk with their fingers, then everyone knows how to move an item around on a touchscreen as well, because it uses the same action. If similar kinds of object always look the same in real life, then similar kinds of objects should always look the same on a screen.

There are of course limits to this, because a user interface is still an abstraction. Apple, ironically enough, attracted criticism a number of years ago for pushing the concept of 'skeuomorphic design' too far. 'Skeuomorphic' simply means that the design of an interface object visually mimics a real-life counterpart – like the recycling bin or trash can that appears on the desktops of most operating systems. But when an interface starts mimicking the grain of wood on book store shelves, or the felt of a gaming table in a game centre (as was the case with the corresponding Apple apps for a number of years), the level of visual noise generated can be distracting.

We will go through some of the specific questions for how to create shared meaning in the next chapter, but when we are faced with so many choices for how best to create shared meaning through visual language, the most important question is 'How do we know?' How do UX designers know that they have created an interface that everyone instinctively knows how to use, and what can we learn from that? While surveys, focus groups and interviews have their place when testing usability, good UX designers know that there is no substitute for actually *watching people using the thing*. Steve Krug defines usability testing as:

> Watching people try to use what you're creating/designing/building (or something you've already created/designed/built), with the intention of (a) making it easier for people to use or (b) proving that it is easy to use.[17]

Think about how often people build visual models of transformation, then stand up and talk through what the model means, assuming that what they are saying and what the model is saying must be in harmony, just because they stem from the same thought process. How do we know that this is the case? What happens when the slide is printed off and put on a wall, or e-mailed to a colleague who wasn't in the presentation? Will it still mean the same thing?

In our experience, the only real way to test what a model means to different audience groups is to get real people from each of those groups, show them a printout of the model, ask them what it means, and then spend the next 5 or 10 minutes listening *without interrupting*. As we have been saying, no model is going to mean exactly the same thing to everyone, but you will invariably find completely unexpected seams of meaning that people tap into, based on the visual choices you have made. This can be a very confronting thing to do; no one likes to feel criticised for something they have spent a lot of time working on, and it's very tempting to rush in and 'defend' your work by explaining the 'real' meaning. But the longer you can hold back, the more you will learn, not just for the current iteration of the model but for your future ability to create shared meaning.

Understand user goals

The second principle from UX design is that it is goal directed. Interaction designer Alan Cooper, Robert Reimann and David Cronin have expressed this well:

> If we design and construct products in such a way that the people who use them achieve their goals, these people will be satisfied, effective, and happy and will gladly pay for the products and recommend that others do the same. Assuming that this can be achieved in a cost-effective manner, it will translate into business success.[18]

This sounds incredibly obvious, and digital interfaces have certainly come on a long way in achieving this since these words were written over a decade ago. Yet plenty of software is still what Cooper and his co-authors describe as 'rude', posting incomprehensible error messages that blame users for problems that are not their fault ('Warning: An unknown error occurred'), and luring them into making significant mistakes that they later regret. When software impedes rather than supports people in achieving their goals, it leads to dissatisfaction, ineffectiveness and irritation.

The reason this happens can again be described using the Continuum. When software is made by people on the bottom right of the Continuum, who have deep expertise in how computers work, they often expect users to behave more like computers than human beings.

The same thing is true of producers of visual models. Earlier in the chapter we talked about the need to ensure that the subject matter of the model aligns with the cares and concerns of the intended audience, but this is already a well-understood principle, reflected, for example, in the concept of views and viewpoints used by business and systems architects (and discussed in Chapter 7). What UX design teaches us is that we need to move beyond this, to understand not just the cares and concerns of our audiences but also the goals that they want to achieve. If we give someone a model, what do we expect them to do with it? What will they be able to do differently as a result? Which conversations will they use it to stimulate, and to what end?

Too often, these questions are only asked *after* the model has been made. UX designers start with these questions, often spending more time consulting with end users and producing mock-ups than they do designing the finished product.

There is clearly a balance to be struck here, as the visuals made during transformation are, for the most part, temporary scaffolding rather than the actual product, but if shared meaning is a pre-requisite for successful change, then surely these kinds of questions should be asked more often?

Views of the future

When we first introduced the Visualisation Continuum as a concept in Chapter 1, we made the observation that there was a 'conspicuous' gap to the top right. We alluded to 'top-right' models earlier in this chapter in the context of BIM. The ideal for visually modelling change would be to find a mechanism that combines the accuracy of the bottom right with the shared meaning of the top left. We will close this chapter with two short case studies of two new approaches that aim to achieve this.

Enterprise design

Milan Guenther introduced the Enterprise Design framework in his book *Intersection*.[19]

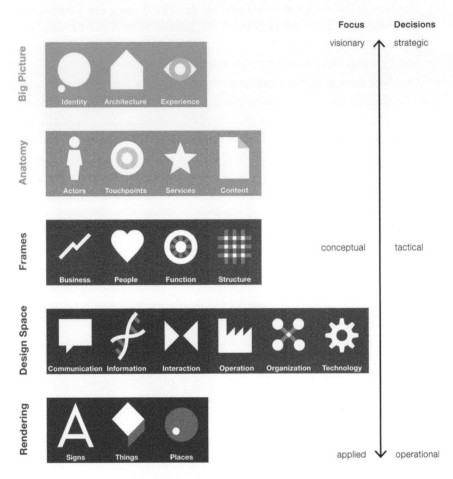

Figure 8.13 The Enterprise Design stack
Reproduced with permission from Milan Guenther.

Milan approaches the challenge of business change with the training and perspective of a designer, but the sensibility of an enterprise architect. The 20 elements of the framework shown in Figure 8.13 form a stack over five layers, from the more abstract, strategic elements at the top to the physical reification of the design at the bottom:

A key objective of the Enterprise Design framework … is to apply a holistic and global view to the complex environment that design projects face in the enterprise. As opposed to purely user-centred, business-driven, service-oriented, or similar design paradigms, it aims to provide a vocabulary and approach without imposing a particular focus or main area of interest. That combination of non-focus and a wide range of aspects covered is based on the central idea of taking into account everything that matters, of overcoming the silos, biases and preconceptions that appear naturally in any multidisciplinary team or diversified stakeholder community.[20]

The core elements constitute a shared language, used in models that would typically otherwise be created by different communities using different methodologies (e.g. business process maps, experience maps, stakeholder maps, empathy maps). Figure 8.14 is an example of the framework elements used to mark up a user persona template.

What is most interesting for our purposes, though, is how the framework has been enhanced by the creation of Enterprise Design Modelling Language (EDML), an evolution of the stack elements into a standards-based visual language, akin to the kinds of architectural languages (such as ArchiMate) that we met in Chapter 7. Unlike those languages, however, EDML has an extremely small vocabulary (three elements to cover entities, activities and qualities) and set of relations (relatedness, sequence and composition). There is no need for a highly developed abstract visual language as there is already so much semantic richness contained in the existing stack elements. The objective is to find an optimum balance between accuracy and shared meaning, without having to sacrifice one or the other outright. An example is given in Figure 8.15; the rectangular shapes represent entities, the chevrons activities and the curved rectangles qualities, with the icons referencing the ontology of the Enterprise Design stack.

The Milky Way method

The Milky Way method was developed in 2013 by Annika Klyver and is documented in a book of the same name by her colleague Cecilia Nordén (2018).[21] It is based on the creation, development and analysis of a single large-scale map of the enterprise that ties together all the other architectural models in a way that is easy for the rest of the business to relate to; see the example in Figure 8.16. This map can then be adapted, experimented with, and overlaid with relevant data to explore patterns and stimulate dialogue.

Figure 8.14 A user persona illustrated using the Enterprise Design framework

Reproduced with permission from Milan Guenther.

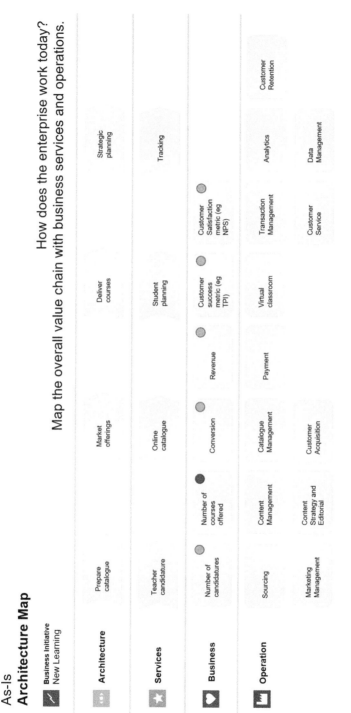

Figure 8.15 A simple high-level EDML model

Reproduced with permission from Milan Guenther.

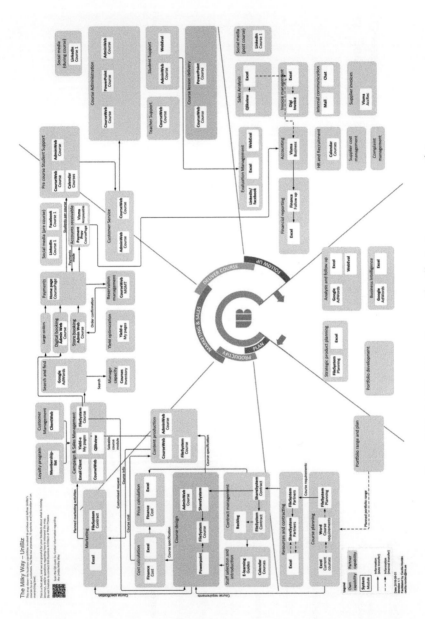

Figure 8.16 A Milky Way diagram (for illustrative purposes only)
Reproduced with permission from Annika Klyver.

Milky Way maps have the following structure:

- A central hub that displays the main steps of the value stream as a series of radial arcs. These elements then demarcate the areas on the rest of the page;
- A series of grey boxes that represent the capabilities required to deliver the value at each stage;
- White boxes representing the IT systems and applications used by each capability;
- Arrows showing the flow of information between capabilities.

We showed an example of a bespoke capability model in Chapter 7 (Figure 7.17). As with that diagram, the Milky Way map exists as an 'anchor model', one that many different types of information can be laid on top of, and that can be adapted and experimented with in order to rapidly try out different potential operating models, while still having everything on one piece of paper. Capability tends to be a good level of abstraction from which to build a 'base model' of organisation, being sufficiently concrete for people to understand what is being talked about, but sufficiently abstract to allow rapid experimentation with alternative models.

As can be seen in Figure 8.17, these models can get extremely detailed (within the constraints of an A0 printer!), not just because the capability modelling becomes richer, but because of the amount of information people want to see overlaid: heatmaps of problematic areas, demarcation of roles and responsibilities, KPIs, product/service flow, change initiatives, project lifecycles, budgets, channels, strategic priorities, technical architecture and so on.

The important thing to recognise is that the consistency of the visual language is what is providing the anchor here: people may be unfamiliar with the finer details of the capabilities, but everyone should have a basic understanding of the value chain and where they fit into it. Therefore, no matter how much information is overlaid onto the picture, the central value stream hub is always central, clearly demarcated and visually salient due to the surrounding white space. For a visual artefact to act as an anchor, it has to not move.

Compare this to the complex IT system example we saw back in Chapter 6 (Figure 6.2), where the conventions used in the picture were

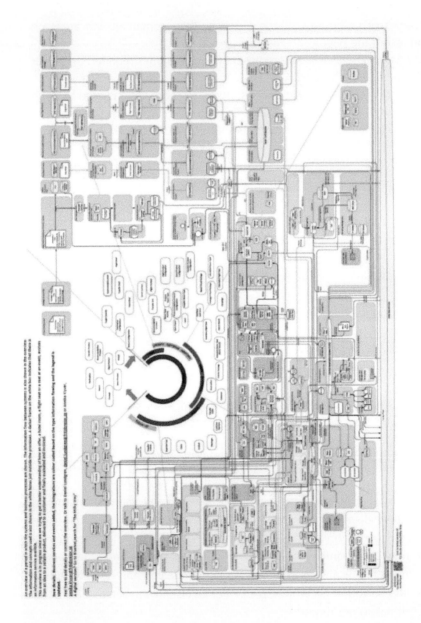

Figure 8.17 A detailed Milky Way diagram (for illustrative purposes only)

Reproduced with permission from Annika Klyver.

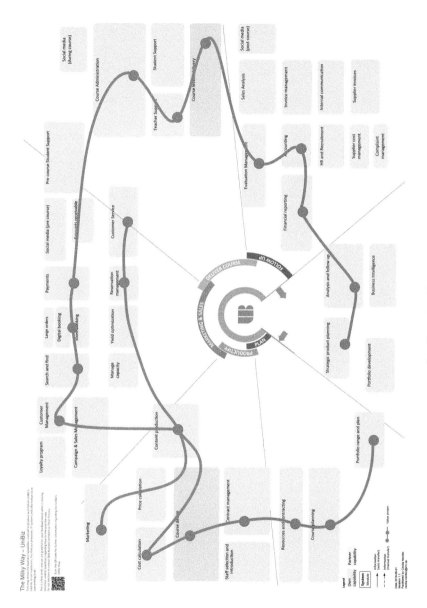

Figure 8.18 A value flow (for illustrative purposes only)
Reproduced with permission from Annika Klyver.

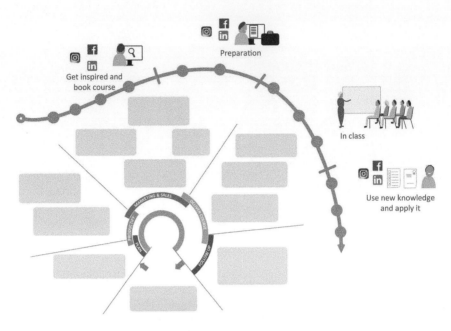

Figure 8.19 A customer journey

Reproduced with permission from Annika Klyver.

idiosyncratic to the creator of the model. Meaning in such models does not tend to travel very far. The Milky Way model, by contrast, with its simple, consistent and recognisable layout and central visual device, can also be the anchor for other perspectives, such as the value flows and customer journey shown in Figures 8.18 and 8.19 respectively.

Notes

1 Krakauer, David. (November 13, 2016). *Complexity & Stupidity*, podcast transcript, https://samharris.org/complexity-stupidity/, accessed July 29, 2019.
2 Ibid.
3 Hegarty, J. (2011). *Hegarty on Advertising*. London: Thames and Hudson.
4 Kotter, J. and Cohen, D. (2002). *The Heart of Change*. Boston, MA: Harvard Business School Press.
5 Graves, Tom. (2013). Enterprise as Story, Enterprise as System, in Gotze and Jensen-Ward (Eds.), *Beyond Alignment: Applying Systems Thinking in Architecting*. London: College Publications, p. 231.

6 Duffy, Francis quoted in Brand, S. (2013). *How Buildings Learn*. Penguin Books, p. 17.

7 BIM by GRAPHISOFT ARCHICAD. Inspired by the Johnson WAX HQ, architect Frank Lloyd Wright.

8 Simon Wardley, licensed under CC BY 4.0 (https://creativecommons.org/licenses/by/4.0/).

9 https://medium.com/wardleymaps/finding-a-path-cdb1249078c0, accessed July 29, 2019.

10 The model can be viewed at http://eu.opmodel.guide, accessed July 29, 2019.

11 A live example of this technology, illustrating the operating model of the European Union is available at http://eu.opmodel.guide.

12 Hayakawa, S. I. (1978). *Language in Thought and Action*. Enlarged ed. San Diego, CA: Harcourt Brace Jovanovich. Originally published as *Language in Action*.

13 Mayer, R. E. (2001). *Multimedia Learning*. Cambridge: Cambridge University Press.

14 Norman, D. (2010). *System Thinking: A Product Is More Than the Product* – extracted from https://jnd.org/systems_thinking_a_product_is_more_than_the_product/. Originally published in *Interactions*, 16(5).

15 Interbrand World's Best Global Brands reports, 2013–2018. https://www.interbrand.com/best-brands/best-global-brands/previous-years/.

16 Krug, S. (2000). *Don't Make Me Think*. New Riders.

17 Krug, S. (2019). *Rocket Surgery Made Easy*. Berkeley, CA: New Riders, p. 13.

18 Cooper, A., Reimann, R. and Cronin, D. (2007). *About Face 3: The Essentials of Interaction Design*. Indianapolis, IN: Wiley, p. 3.

19 Guenther, M. (2013). *Intersection*. Amsterdam: Elsevier/Morgan Kufmann.

20 Ibid., p. 234.

21 Nordén, Cecilia. (2018). *The Milky Way: Map, Navigate and Accelerate Change*. IRM.

9 Using visual language effectively

Maximising shared meaning

At this point it may sound like the solution to creating shared meaning is simply to 'descend the ladder' (see Figure 8.10), to whatever degree that is culturally and financially possible. But we all know that not all visualisations are created equal. The mere fact that you spend money on a video or an interactive game to explain a complex set of concepts doesn't mean that the video or the game will be any good! Having an artist in a room drawing a picture while the group describes a vision and journey adds no value if the resulting picture bears no resemblance to what people are talking about, or if it is rolled up and never looked at again.

We should also repeat the point that visualisation is not the only way to create shared meaning. If the relevant concepts can be communicated by just changing the way we use words (e.g. telling stories, giving examples, using metaphors, etc.) then that will always be more efficient. Our focus in this book though is on the kind of inter-connected, non-linear, systemic concepts that tend to be the focal point of organisational change and are almost impossible to communicate using words alone.

So how could organisations *learn* to make better use of visual language in a way that creates shared meaning? There are many books and training courses aimed at getting corporate citizens to draw more pictures (as discussed in Chapter 4). This is a great place to start – simply helping people get over their fear of drawing can start a cultural shift down the ladder. Making it okay for employees to ask colleagues from other silos 'Can you draw that for me?' is bound to have a compound effect that increases overall organisational agility over time, simply by increasing the shared meaning across boundaries.

198

This is not a book on drawing and visual design, so we will not spend time here repeating these kinds of techniques and exercises. Zooming out to the overall process of model production though, there are some fundamental questions to ask in order to maximise the level of shared meaning obtained from visualisation:

- Are the elements represented familiar to the audience?
- Are the elements represented in an experiential way?
- Are the metaphors familiar?
- Are the principles of visual perception applied?
- Does the appearance harmonise with the structure?

We will look at each of these in turn.

Are the elements represented familiar to the audience?

The first test, clearly, is whether anyone in the audience actually has any experience of what is being represented! The most clear and elegant visual model of the inner workings of a database management system will mean nothing to someone with no idea what a database is.

This may seem like common sense, but it's always worth checking that the 'curse of knowledge'[1] is not affecting our judgement of what people know. One of the most basic principles of User Interface (UI) testing is not to tell the test subjects anything about how the interface works, but simply to observe what they do. It's surprising how often users misinterpret what the UI is even for.

Similarly, when testing visual models, we have found it always worthwhile to show a sample audience a draft without giving them any introduction or context, and ask them to say what *they* think it means. The results can be very surprising!

Are the elements represented in an experiential way?

All other things being equal, the more an element *looks like* the thing it represents, the likelier it will be to create shared meaning.

In following this principle, we experience the tension we described on the abstraction ladder between effectiveness and efficiency: adding pictures, photographs or similar 'experiential' content helps viewers orient to things they already know, but is 'costly' in that it uses up precious space on the page. This reinforces the point made above that we need to be clear which concepts are the highest priority for people to understand in order to have meaningful conversations. This prioritisation should determine the size, location and presence of visual elements on the page.

Are the metaphors familiar?

We mentioned in Chapter 4 the danger of over-using creative metaphors during rich picture design: metaphors that mean more to those in the workshop developing the picture than to the audience it is supposed to be making sense for. There is a tension between the meaning 'inside the room', where the picture is being developed and the meaning 'outside the room' once it is finished.

Metaphor is a pervasive feature of human psychology – we constantly make sense of the world by comparing things to what they are not, even when we are not aware that we are doing so. All metaphors share the same structure: there is a source domain from which we extract meaning and a target domain to which we apply it. So, for example, if we say 'the competition is coming towards us like a bulldozer',[2] the source domain is the bulldozer and the target domain is the competition. The important thing to realise is that we always do this comparison *selectively*. The relevant source features of a bulldozer are presumably its strength, ability to destroy, and the slow and steady movement in a single direction. The majority of the source features are not transferred though – we are almost certainly not saying that the competition has caterpillar-tracked wheels, a single-occupancy cabin, high CO_2 emissions, etc.

We can think of metaphors as existing on a spectrum from the creative to the conventional. Creative metaphors are those that immediately stand out to us as metaphors, for example: 'What light through yonder window breaks? It is the east, and Juliet is the sun.' Conventional metaphors are those that pepper our speech without us noticing: 'We have a close relationship with our customers.' The more conventional the metaphor, the more likely it is to create shared meaning, because the association is already embedded in the language.

While creative metaphors are associated with rich pictures and other creative illustrations, conventional metaphors crop up everywhere, including in simple diagrams. If two elements are vertically arranged, for example, we will conventionally assume that the higher one has more power, importance or strength than the lower one. Elements that are close together will be assumed to have a close association.

Conventional metaphors, once understood, are a great way of ensuring shared meaning, because they tend to mean the same for different people. It's worth pointing out though that if you are at the sense-making phase of transformation, your purpose may be the opposite of shared meaning; you may want to get as great a diversity of ideas on the table as possible. The brain is infinitely supple in its ability to draw meaning out of unlikely comparisons, so having small groups commit to full-blooded exploration of analogies at the creative end of the metaphor spectrum is one of the fastest ways to generate fresh insights, especially with an artist in the room reflecting back the imagery that's implied.

Nevertheless, the same rules apply in that there has to be some level of shared meaning for the conversation to be possible. Crucially, participants need to be committed to exploring the meaning in other people's metaphors rather than just imposing their own, for any higher order insights to emerge. An excellent approach to this, grounded in metaphor theory, is Caitlin Walker's Systemic Modelling methodology,[3] which applies clean language (a metaphorical modelling technique) to group settings.

Are the principles of visual perception applied?

In creating shared meaning, it's important to be aware of the commonalities in how people perceive visual structures. As an example, the Gestalt principles (enumerated in the first half of the twentieth century) suggest a series of rules that the brain applies in order to distinguish one thing from another. Examples of the main principles are shown in Figure 9.1.

In each example, the eye automatically combines elements in order to deduce what the thing is that is being looked at. The rule explains the principle that is being applied – elements are combined when they are

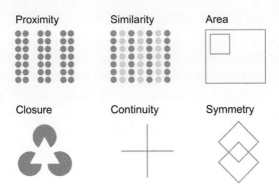

Figure 9.1 Example Gestalt principles

close together, similar, following a continuous pattern, can be enclosed, fall within an area, or are symmetrical.

Gestalt psychology[4] is just one well-known example of a visual theory, and there are many books and articles available for those who want to pursue this further. We include it here as an example to make a broader point, which is that graphical designers are typically taught these principles whereas business people and consultants are not.

What difference would it make, for example, if the creator of a metamodel in an enterprise architecture team understood and could embody these principles of visual perception in their work? How much larger a potential audience could exist for technical reference models if they were easier for non-technical colleagues to read?

Does the appearance harmonise with the structure?

We have made a number of references in this book to Alex Osterwalder's Business Model Canvas, probably the best known and most used business diagram of the past decade. Very few people, however, have studied Osterwalder's PhD thesis, from which the model is derived. It's interesting to compare the ontological model in the thesis (Figure 9.2) with the visual model that is now commonly seen (Figure 9.3).

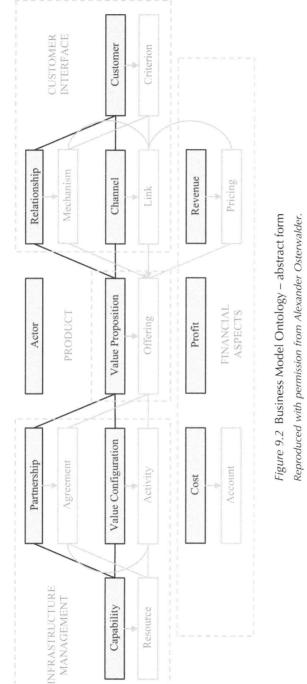

Figure 9.2 Business Model Ontology – abstract form

Reproduced with permission from Alexander Osterwalder.

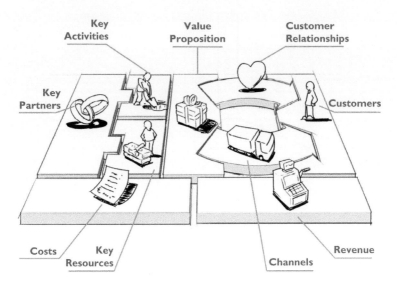

Figure 9.3 Business Model Canvas – experiential form

Reproduced with permission from John Wiley & Sons.

What immediately becomes obvious is that the visual representation is in harmony with the underlying conceptual structure. For example:

- The distinction between vertical and horizontal blocks has meaning: vertical blocks represent delivery elements, whereas horizontal blocks represent financial elements;
- Size of gaps between blocks has meaning: the gap that the arrows fit in represents an organisational separation between producer and consumer;
- Interconnections have meaning: notice the tabs on the left, which represent collaboration;
- The icons have meaning, acting as a mental shortcut to the concepts they represent.

In our experience of observing the kinds of models created and used within organisations, this level of 'resonance' (discussed at greater length in Chapter 5) between conceptual and visual is vanishingly rare. More typical is for concepts of completely different ontological types to be spread randomly across the page, as in Figure 9.4.

Looking ahead: Our strategic review

Service Delivery Model	Health & Safety	Commission-ing and control
Governance C of C	Vision	Ind Relations
Customer Satisfaction	Innovation	5-year plan

Figure 9.4 Typical slideware example

The trouble in most organisations is that the visual representation and the conceptual structure are created by different teams. On the one hand there are graphics teams, designers, live artworkers, communications professionals, and on the other hand are managers, change professionals, consultants and so on. What might it mean in practice for an organisation to bring the two sides back together?

For visual professionals, it could mean getting the space and time to ask the kinds of questions that get to the bottom of what concepts actually *mean*, before depicting them visually. It could mean learning some of the technical language and modelling techniques that domain experts use – 'climbing the ladder' of abstraction within a given silo in order to create artefacts that are more meaningful to those outside it.

For content holders it could mean picking up a book on design and learning visual language principles, so as to be able to have more meaningful conversations with designers about layout decisions. It could mean testing content 'blind', as we suggested earlier, to see if audiences from different domains interpret the models in the same way. It would certainly mean learning to restrict the amount of content included in each model, so that the designer has some flexibility in how the elements are arranged.

These are just the start. We described in the previous section the need to break down silos in order to achieve organisational agility through shared meaning. Perhaps the division between visual professionals (who spend their time making pictures) and content holders (who spend their time writing words) would be a good place to start.

Notes

1 A cognitive bias that occurs when an individual, communicating with other individuals, unknowingly assumes that the others have the background to understand.
2 Making a distinction between similes and metaphors serves little purpose for visualisation: they are grammatically distinct examples of the same cognitive phenomenon.
3 Walker, C. (2014). *From Contempt to Curiosity*. Portchester: Clean Publishing.
4 See, for example, https://en.wikipedia.org/wiki/Gestalt_psychology, accessed July 29, 2019.

10 Epilogue

If we were to sum up our observations from working on this book together, it would be that visualisation builds bridges, which is good news for those working on transformation, which can be one of the most rending experiences you can have.

It is perhaps surprising that the implementation of business change has not drawn more attention from sociologists and anthropologists, as it provides some fascinating insights into how people get driven apart. Groups of high-functioning individuals come together for a limited time to achieve a common aim, but each group and individual, from inside and outside the organisation, has their own language, culture, specialism, prejudices and (often) employer. They are all expected to put their natural biases and allegiances to one side in pursuit of a shared goal.

Most of the splintering arises from how this coalition itself deals with change, because the situation is never static: in terms of people, programme leadership changes hands whenever progress targets aren't being met, sponsorship is moved as senior executives come and go, and consultancy partners arrive and depart as they come into and out of favour. In terms of content, requirements are constantly re-evaluated, the aim is rarely understood in the same way by everyone, and although everyone desperately wants to succeed, most people know that pretty much no large-scale transformation ever lives up to the hype of its original business case.

In the midst of all this change, everyday human dynamics are playing out. Individual contractors are on day rates, and want to show that they are worth them. Teams will often (consciously or unconsciously) use deliberately vague language in their early reports in order to avoid being tied down to specific commitments later on. If a new team member uses some in-vogue jargon in a meeting, it can be hard to tell if that person is trying to make a serious point, or just wants to sound more like an expert. If it emerges that the programme's executive sponsor is ill-informed, insufficiently skilled or has misunderstood the issues affecting it, the programme team has to soldier on regardless. Then there are the small-scale skirmishes that occur between projects competing for the same funds or senior leadership favour, between different philosophies (agile vs waterfall, systemic vs reductionist, user-centric vs enterprise-centric, etc.), or between change managers and technical specialists trying to build relationships with the same key stakeholders.

For our sociologists and anthropologists to truly understand why this situation, established to draw people together, so rapidly drives them apart, they would need to be joined by another group: linguists. This is because all of these forces have one effect in common: they fragment meaning – not by design but by consequence.

In a complex transformation involving hundreds of people, where the change itself keeps evolving, it is incredibly hard to maintain shared meaning across all constituencies. It is almost inevitable that shared meaning will fragment down to the level of each participant's local team, where everyone at least has the shared reference points of common specialisms and common experiences. Over time, each team builds its own model of what's going on, what everyone's motivation is, who can be trusted, who 'gets it', what needs to be done; yet all of these perceptions are expressed and only make sense in the language of the team that generates them.

These kinds of problems are typically put down to lack of inter-team communication, but without some shared reference points to start with, this can have the opposite effect. The meaning of words is a construction of the people who are hearing or reading them, so unless each team member can break out of their prior mental models to see the world from the other's point of view, interaction across teams can just serve to reinforce prejudices. When projects are under pressure (which they usually are!), the stress and tensions make it far likelier that we will hear what we expect to hear, rather than what the other person is trying to say.

It's hardly a new observation that pictures can help solve these problems. Everyone, after all, has heard the old adage (which we have managed to scrupulously avoid up to this point!) that 'a picture tells a thousand words'. Visualisation works because pictures are closer to our experience of everyday life than words, and the fastest way to create shared meaning is to create symbols that connect with shared experiences of what's important to people.

For most of the book we have demonstrated this with reference to what we've called the Visualisation Continuum, and in relation to the unspoken force that tends to pull technical teams (delivering the nuts and bolts) away from change, and communications and user-engagement teams that are trying to bring the rest of the organisation along on the journey.

The conclusion we have come to is simple and obvious, and stems from the fact that more often than not both sides are *trying to describe the same things* and *trying to achieve the same things*. We need to have more humility and more curiosity for those who see the world in different ways to us. What would it be like for a trained graphic facilitator to learn UML and hang out with technical architects? What would it be like for a business process analyst to become fluent in creating rich pictures? What new technologies could be produced if we put shared meaning across the Continuum as a design objective in its own right?

In conclusion, the point we want to make here is that although we have framed the book in the light of our own experiences of change, and our own personal positions at either end of the Continuum, the principles have broader application. By visualising what we mean, we connect abstract concepts to shared experiences and in doing so build bridges of shared meaning. This is not just true for enterprise architects talking to change consultants, but also for representatives of different organisational departments, different employers, different specialisms, different job grades, different backgrounds. Indeed, it's not just true for organisations and organisational change, but for change at all levels across the world.

Our hope is that wherever you see yourself on the spectrum, whatever your background and preferred language, you will have had your curiosity piqued by how others represent change visually, and that your own world will be enriched with new possibilities as a result.

Index

Page numbers in italics refer to figures